101 WAYS TO MAKE
MORE SPACE
STYLISH HOME IDEAS

Hylas Publishing
Publisher: Sean Moore
Creative Director: Karen Prince
Designer: Gus Yoo

First Published in 2004 by
BBC Worldwide Ltd,
Woodlands, 80 Wood Lane, London W12 0TT
All photographs © BBC *Good Homes* with the
exception of: Ideal Standard 51, 53; Hillary's
Blinds 95, 97, 151, 163, 165; Cosyfloor 152;
Bisque 153; Roundhouse Kitchens and
Bartholomew Conservatories 159; Dominic
Blackmore 149.

Published in the United States by
Hylas Publishing
129 Main Street, Irvington,
New York 10533

Copyright © BBC Worldwide 2004

The moral right of the author has been asserted.

ISBN 1-59258-071-8

Commissioning Editor: Vivien Bowler
Project Editor: Rebecca Hardie
Series Design: Claire Wood
Book Design: Kathryn Gammon
Design Manager: Annette Peppis
Production Controller: Arlene Alexander

First American Edition published in 2003
02 03 04 05 10 9 8 7 6 5 4 3 2 1

Set in Amasis MT and ITC Officina Sans

Color origination by Radstock Reproductions
Ltd, Midsomer Norton

Distributed by St. Martin's Press

101 WAYS TO MAKE MORE SPACE

STYLISH HOME IDEAS

Julie Savill

HYLAS
PUBLISHING

BBC

CONTENTS

INTRODUCTION   6

VISUAL TRICKS   8   KITCHEN AND BATH   22

DOUBLE UP   60   DIVIDE AND RULE   86

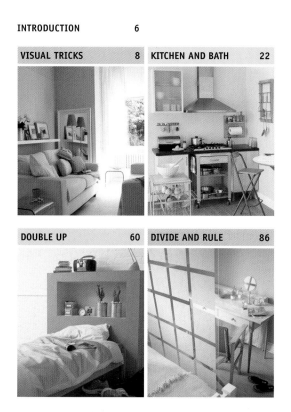

SORT AND STORE   100

PLANNING SPACE   138

ADDITIONS   158

QUICK FIXES   168

WHERE TO BUY   210

INTRODUCTION

There are very few people who could put their hand on their heart and say they have enough space in their home. Whether it's kids arriving or growing up, a new need for a home office or an active social life that demands lots of entertaining the pressures on the space in our homes just seem to grow and grow. Couple that with today's desire for an airy, light and laid-back look and it's immediately obvious that some clever design ideas are needed to achieve all we want from the homes we have.

A good tidy-up is the starting point and it's quite eye-opening just how much more roomy a place can seem if the floor and furniture are clear of clutter. Of course, clutter can be the result of a lack of storage leaving no permanent home for belongings and this should be the next step – creating a place for everything, which is the only way you'll ever persuade the family to put things in their place. If you have enough rooms but they are of mean proportion a little light trickery is what's called for. Color, pattern, mirror and light can all be brought into play to trick the eye into thinking spaces are longer, wider, taller, lighter and brighter giving you a sense of space way beyond the real boundaries of your rooms. Of course, tidying up and chucking out the old newspapers isn't going to give you the extra bedroom you need or create the space you want for the family to gather and enjoy cooking and eating together. But, before you opt for the upheaval of building work or moving to a bigger place, it does pay to consider how you use the rooms you already have. Ask yourself if you are using every space to the full; is there a room which could be divided temporarily or permanently to make separate areas for different tasks or people; would different furniture let you eke a little more use out of the space you already have?

If there's nothing else for it and the walls have got to move for you, take heart. An addition can often work out cheaper than moving house, particularly when the housing market is buoyant, as you'll be saving not only the cost of upgrading to a bigger property but also all the associated costs such as solicitors and removals companies. And if you like where you live why move and uproot everyone when a bigger home is just an addition away.

Julie Savill, Editor

Clever color

Wield the paintbrush to correct oddly proportioned rooms with an optical illusion.

Ceiling: Ceilings aren't traditionally painted white for nothing. So before you decide to break the mould and opt for a color, consider the fact that anything deeper than a shade of cream will make the ceiling appear lower and darken the room overall.

Walls: Painting your walls in bands of different colors will add visual interest to a room and can be used to trick the eye into thinking a space is wider or generally bigger than it actually is. A horizontal band of darker color taken to dado height will immediately make a room seem wider. In a tall space you can afford to use a similar shade on the ceiling to exaggerate the effect even more. Take the darker color up to picture-rail height with a band of a paler shade above and a classic white ceiling, and you keep the feeling of width but gain an impression of height, making the space seem bigger in all directions.

Flooring: The pale golden tones of this laminate flooring complement the light, airy feel of the room. The narrow boards were chosen deliberately to make the floor area seem more extensive. Adding a rug would break up the floor space and add welcome warmth.

Furniture: A folding table makes a neat four-seater for everyday family dining but flips out an extra leaf to seat six people comfortably for entertaining. Chairs with spindly legs allow a clear line of sight under the table adding to the sense of space.

The big sleep

Stripes play a major part in changing the appearance of a room with nothing more than a splash of color.

Vertical: Just as you can use stripes in fashion to create a longer, leaner look, bands of vertical painted color on your walls will make them seem to stretch skywards. Choose coordinating shades rather than high contrast colors to avoid making the room seem chaotic. Broad stripes work but the narrower the stripe the greater the effect will be. This technique is to be avoided at all costs in rooms with very high ceilings as it will create a tunnel effect.

Horizontal: Turn the stripes on their side and this will appear to stretch the space widthways. Try this on just one wall – the one facing you as you enter a room is ideal – if you feel it would be too much all round. As with the vertical stripes, the impression is greater with narrower stripes. Horizontal stripes will make the ceiling appear lower so are best used in taller rooms.

Shine: A sophisticated, subtle but effective way to use this technique is to alternate bands of matt and shiny paint in the same color. The play of light on the different surfaces will bring you all the benefits of the colored stripes but in a more understated way that's probably better suited to living rooms.

TIP

With this much color and pattern interest in a room, the furniture and furnishings need to be kept perfectly plain and simple. White is your best ally for adding calm and pleasing freshness.

Add highlights

Light, bright shades are the best choice to make the most of a space but for a pale scheme to be interesting it must have a range of tones and textures.

Color: To make a room look larger use pale colors on the walls, floors, ceiling and in the furnishings. Pale, cool colors like watery greens, blues and white are called receding colors because they visually push walls away from you. These colors reflect the light, whereas dark colors tend to absorb light. Pure white can look clinically cold (and diabolically dirty if you have small children). Opt instead for not-quite-whites: warm creams, pebbly colors or color-tinted whites which will still give you the space-enhancing qualities of white but will be more liveable.

Contrast: In this room the color interest is supplied by the honey-colored timber and textural contrasts of silky versus woolly fabrics. The bed is neatly made with a knitted throw, a sheeny satin quilt and crisp cotton sheets that invite you in.

Furniture: The bed itself is a clever choice for a small room. The platform top allows plenty of room for sleeping and resting books and drinks along the side. As it is cantilevered out over the base the effect is lighter than a traditional solid divan base. Low-level furniture such as this is ideal in a room with a low ceiling as it helps even out the proportions.

Finishing touch: Not a trick has been missed in this room. The long picture shelf with its timber-framed photos lends a strong horizontal line to the room that makes it seem wider than it really is.

Every trick in the book

This room is a perfect example of making the most of a less than generously sized room.

Color: The wall color is pale but interesting and goes right up to picture-rail height giving a lofty feel to the space. A contrast shade above is of a similar tone so it doesn't dominate. Everything else in the room is kept deliberately pale and manages to avoid cramping the room even though it is full of furniture and accessories.

Tables: Ditch the central coffee table and keep a walkway clear through the room so you can see an expanse of carpet when you enter. Small side tables are a better idea and can be positioned for comfortable use wherever you sit in the room. So much the better if they are a nesting set which will tuck into a corner. Choose Perspex or glass furniture and it will blend into the background.

Seating: Sofas and armchairs raised on legs create a sense of space and light as you can see the carpet stretching away underneath them.

Mirror: Take a tip from a professional stylist and simply prop a large mirror casually against a wall. The angle of the mirror will give a new dimension to the reflection.

Window: Fine and wispy voile drapes at the window maximize the natural light but still offer plenty of privacy.

TIP
Don't forget the tables will be turned at night when lamps are lit and those outside will be able to see in if you have voile curtains – double up with a neat roller blind.

Fade away

Love one color? Use it everywhere and see how it makes your home grow.

Walls: Start with the strongest shade in the hub of your home – the hall. It will create an impact as you enter and if the rooms off it are all of paler shades they will appear to open out in front of you. For each room select a different, paler shade of your chosen color but don't feel you have to be entirely rigid with your selection. In this yellow scheme, adjoining rooms could go as pale as cream or even white or acquire a hint of green with more limey shades.

Ceilings: Use the color on the wall up to picture-rail height then paint the ceilings in sparkling white or palest cream. Bring the ceiling shade down to meet the wall color to give an impression of lofty space.

Bedding: Reserve the palest shade of your chosen color for the bedlinen to minimize the impact the bed has on the space. If your bed has pretty legs leave off the valance to allow a view underneath (but only if it's tidy down there!).

Floor: Ratty carpet isn't 'top of the style' but if you can't afford to replace it, there are other options. Rip up the carpet and underlay and inspect the floorboards below. If they are in great condition simply sand them back to pale wood and lime or varnish them. If they've been repaired at any point or are very stained and pitted, fill the holes with wood filler then cover the lot with two or three coats of specialist floor paint in bright white. The glossy surface will make the room sparkle with light and is wonderfully easy to clean.

Cool tones

Subtlety is the key if you want to create a room with lots of interest and a feeling of space, air and calm.

Color: Pale grey shades are fashionable, sophisticated and wonderfully cool. When used in a confined space they will have the effect of making the walls seem further away. Stick to a palette of two or three very similar shades and it's possible to build delicate tonal schemes that will work wonders on a room's proportions. Allow yourself a flash of exotic color in the flowers on the table.

Proportion: If a room is long and narrow paint the wall at the far end in the slightly darker tone to make it seem to come towards you. If a room is wide and shallow, reverse the colors with the darker shade on the side walls to draw them in and the paler shade on the other walls to make them recede.

Flooring: Laminate or wooden flooring can also be used to change your impression of the size of a room. Lay it with the boards running across the room to make it seem wider, or the length of the room, away from the door, to make it seem longer.

Mirror: A full-length mirror propped casually against the wall mimics the effect of an open door giving the impression that you are catching a glimpse into an adjoining room.

Furniture: A huge shelving unit along one wall provides a whole bank of storage but in its original wooden finish was an overwhelming element in the room. Repainted in the same shade as the wall behind, it is less dominant.

Reflected glory

A hall grows in stature with the careful placing of a huge sheet of mirror.

Mirror: Although this hall isn't tiny it is awkwardly shaped and the stairs come to an end opposite an expanse of blank wall making it feel enclosed and claustrophobic. By positioning a single vast mirror on the wall facing the foot of the stairs the view is opened out giving a far more spacious effect as you descend. Taking the mirror from skirting to ceiling maximizes the effect as the edges are lost in the corners of the recess and there is nothing to remind you that it is simply a reflection and not the real thing.

Color: An off-white on the walls gives the room Scandinavian airiness and is taken up and over the ceiling and cornice for continuity. A very pale grey has been chosen to highlight the staircase. The only pattern relieving the plainness of the scene comes from the natural skeleton leaves which have been glued to the wall at random intervals.

Flooring: Large squares of creamy limestone on the floor help to play up the room's dimensions. Leaving the tiled floor bare of rugs or carpets only serves to make it seem bigger. The tiles have been cut into slices to make a small skirting board around the room which helps to trick the eye into thinking the floor is slightly larger than it is.

TIP
Use spray adhesive to fix skeleton leaves or feathers to walls. Choose a repositionable type and you'll be able to remove them without damaging the paint underneath.

Shine on

In your quest for a home that looks and feels bigger than it really is exploit the fact that shiny surfaces reflect the light and give a reality-busting impression of space.

Tiles: Work the basic trick of using horizontal lines as hard as possible by using slim rows of glass to break up floor to ceiling tiling. Edged with chrome inset strips these narrow border tiles are subtle and stylish but offer just enough contrast to lead the eye horizontally. The sparkly highlights they bring lift the atmosphere without over-whelming the discreet scheme. This type of tile can be expensive but the small amounts needed to enliven a room make them a worthwhile indulgence.

Flooring: The darker tiles on the floor have been brought up the wall in place of a skirting board. The visual effect is to make the floor seem bigger than it is as the eye doesn't immediately pick up the join between wall and floor.

Shelves: Bathroom storage can be bulky and intrusive but by paring down the things that need to be on display and choosing clear glass shelving rather than built-in cabinets you can create a feeling of space beyond your actual square yards. Glass doesn't interrupt the line of sight so has a barely-there quality that's a real bonus in a tight space.

Radiator: Metal finishes are big style news for both kitchens and bathrooms and while it was once big-budget designer luxury, affordable items are now available from department stores — ranges in steel, aluminum or even steel-effect finishes. Chrome is a good ally when you want to make the most of limited space as it reflects even more of that all-important light.

Steel appeal

Awkwardly-shaped rooms need a little extra help if they are to look larger than life.

Space: A sloping ceiling is no barrier to creating a well-planned roomy kitchen. Those odd-shaped areas can be brought into play for all sorts of storage uses. Open shelving is a natural choice as you can simply cut successive shelves shorter as the space gets narrower. In this top-floor flat a cabinet has been designed to fit perfectly under the slope of the ceiling.

Tiles: It's a bit of an indulgence but replacing kitchen tiles with steel ones is a great way to bring those all important reflective surfaces into a kitchen. And after all, if your kitchen is small you won't be talking about yard after yard of tiles. It's unusual in a kitchen to get this sort of shiny finish above worktop height but it works a treat to make even the tiniest kitchen appear to double in size.

Floor: We have 'industrial style' to thank for the popularity of stainless steel in the home. Another look that's borrowed straight from industry is tread plate flooring; with its shiny surface it's a good fit in a metallic kitchen and practical too with a non-slip surface.

TIP
Get the look of tread plate without the headache of cleaning it. Big laminate-flooring specialists are now producing look-alike flooring but with a smooth easy-clean surface.

Check it off

Ease the squeeze in your most-used room with this checklist of tried and tested tricks to make it seem bigger. This room's got virtually the full house.

Open shelving: Use it in place of closed wall cabinets to give an airy feel. There are practical benefits too in that you can see and reach your frequently used items immediately.

Color: Walls in pale colors appear further away than those in dark shades so it pays to think light and bright. Relieve the plainness with small detail such as micro-tiling with a well-spaced geometric design in contrasting colors.

Window: Consider whether you need a window treatment at all. Stripping away curtains and blinds is very liberating if you're not overlooked. If privacy is an issue make sure your chosen treatment hangs inside the window recess or within the extent of the window frame. Roller blinds, Venetian blinds and Roman blinds are all top choices.

Shine: Get those glossy surfaces worked into your scheme and see how the reflected light helps make a space seem bigger. Chrome, steel, glass, gloss laminates, gloss paint and pearlized surfaces will all add to the effect.

Mirror: Sneak a little mirror into an alcove or onto a cabinet door and it not only helps the light level but will also appear to give you a view into another adjoining space.

Slimline storage

In a long, narrow galley kitchen, space is at a premium and you have to think clever to get the most out of the limited area.

Clear walls: A sense of openness and airiness can easily be achieved by dispensing with wall cabinets in favour of clear wall space or shelving and racks. If you don't think you'll have enough cabinet space then clearing the wall cabinets from just one side of the kitchen will make a great deal of difference to the feel of the room.

Base cabinets: Base cabinets are deep and take up a lot of floor space whereas wall cabinets are slimmer and neater. Be honest with yourself and take a good look into your cabinets. Chances are that lurking at the back are all those things you don't use but haven't got around to clearing out. If you are selective about what you store and only hang on to the things that you use regularly or like, then you will probably be able to change your base cabinets for wall cabinets along one side of the kitchen and give yourself at least 8" more floor space.

Racks and shelves: Wall-mounted open storage systems are widely available and much more adaptable than cabinets. Make your kitchen more functional by adding wall racks for the items you use every day, leaving all the cabinet space for longer term storage and for things which would otherwise gather dust.

Window: A Roman blind is the way forward for kitchen windows. Neat and unobtrusive, it will hang within the area of the window frame, taking up less space than curtains and giving a clean, simple line to a window or door.

On the up

A fully functioning kitchen has been worked into a wall run of just 12 feet.

Planning: Several evenings with graph paper and pencil went into working out what went where in this pared-to-the-bone kitchen. In a quest to create a sociable cooking and eating space the kitchen had to remain on just one wall of the room. The range and sink are just far enough apart to have a usable piece of worktop in between and all appliances are hidden behind white doors below.

Style: Plain-fronted cabinets and long lean handles that line up precisely give a streamlined look to the space. In the all-white room, one other color has been worked in. The beech of the worktop is repeated on the floor and the dining table for uniformity and warmth.

Walls: This galley kitchen exploits the storage potential of the high ceilings without looking heavy. The reason? Your eye goes straight to the open shelving and hardly notices the enclosed cabinets above them.

Clever touch: If you are planning a new kitchen don't miss the chance to build in space-creating touches such as a drawer-front that pulls out to reveal a useful extra work surface. Some ranges even incorporate drawers into the plinth area below the cabinets.

Lighting: In this kind of dual-purpose room flexible lighting is a must. When it's time to cook, the posable lights fixed to the top of the wall cabinets cast brilliant white halogen light on the worktop. With these switched off and the room lights dimmed the kitchen area fades into the background leaving a relaxed atmosphere for dining.

Meals on wheels

Proper planning lets you cram lots into even the smallest kitchen. Try these quick tricks.

Furniture: Installing a folding table creates a comfy corner for quick meals, even when you thought there wasn't room. Choose one that is hinged to the wall or make a space for a freestanding table to hang or be tucked away when it's not needed giving you as much free floor space as possible. Folding chairs can get the same treatment, either hanging from hooks or slipping into a cabinet while stacking chairs will just sit neatly in a corner.

Range: Think carefully about how you eat before you splash out on a top-of-the-line range. Do you use an oven? Or is your style of cooking all about the cooktop and the microwave? There's no point in having an oven if you don't use it. Better to invest in a microwave that includes grill and conventional oven options for the rare occasions it's needed. Have a separate cooktop fitted into a run of worktops and use the space underneath for more storage.

Trolleys: Cabinets that slide away under the worktop and pull out when the pressure's on will give you flexibility. A large butcher's block-style trolley that slips under the cooktop can be used to keep pans and bowls right on hand and pulls out to give you an extra work surface.

Colors: Fashion is playing right into your hands at the moment if you are trying to make a compact kitchen seem more spacious. Pale wood cabinets are the way to go. Teamed with crisp, apple green walls it's a winning recipe.

The big breakfast

If a breakfast bar is big on your wish list but your kitchen is on the small side some lateral thinking is called for if you're going to make everything fit.

Storage: Fitting a breakfast bar along a wall will almost always mean losing some cabinet space. A double bank of MDF (medium density fiberglass) box shelves on the wall will go a long way to re-homing the contents of the cabinets and you can take the opportunity to create a visually exciting display of your nicest china and favorite accessories.

Color: Paint the storage system the same color as the wall and it will fade into the background minimizing the visual impact.

Bench: A café-style bar needn't be very deep so it might mean you steal back a little extra floor space. Use a length of oiled beech worktop or a laminated worktop cut down to the right width and screw it to a batten along the back wall with the front edge supported on chrome legs (most hardware stores sell all types of legs for this sort of project). Add a few high bar-stools in fun colors for real diner style.

Messages: Take the chance to incorporate a message area that the whole family can use to keep track of appointments and events. A steel curtain wire screwed in place under the wall cabinets is ideal. Use the curtain clips to fasten pictures, invitations, shopping lists and other reminders.

ABCDEFGHIJKLMNOPQRSTUVWXYZ

Budget special

When you've just bought your first place or upgraded to your first family home there's not always the money to splash out on fancy fittings. But an orderly life can be had on a budget if you do a little customizing.

Base cabinets: Buying the cheapest possible kitchen cabinets means you won't have to stint and can fill the room giving you a clean, smart, well-organized space that will tide you over for the first few years while you save for the kitchen of your dreams. Use a laminate primer on some of the doors and repaint them to give a designer touch.

Walls: Fill the walls with cheap and cheerful open storage and reserve your nicest china, glass and accessories to display here. Seek out basic cube-type storage and simply build the cabinets up into a sleek bank all along one wall. Using them either side of the range hood will give a more integrated and streamlined effect.

Window: A ready-made roller blind fits neatly into the window recess and leaves the window-sill free for your sink-side essentials.

Backsplash: Sheeny metals have good light-reflecting properties that can really give a small space a lift. Here, sheets of galvanized metal have been cut to fit between the wall cabinets and the worktop as a smart backsplash.

TIP

Once your main storage is in place, add extra hanging rails and shelves to fill the gaps but make sure you stick to your overall color scheme to tie all the different elements together.

Less is more

A small square kitchen might be limited in space but it's a great shape to work with.

Layout: A square or nearly square room is just crying out for a U-shaped layout of cabinets and worktops. Standing in the middle of this arrangement means all three sides will be just a step away making it an efficient space to work in. Slightly wider than a traditional galley kitchen, it will also be a comfortable place for two people to share the cooking duties side by side. Having cabinets all around in this way offers masses of work surface so you can afford to have your best-looking accessories, such as a chrome toaster or blender, out on permanent display.

Sink: Place the sink under the window so you have a view, or at least good daylight as you stand there. Having the sink off-center means that one corner of the worktop remains clear as usable work space. The corner to the right of the sink can then be home to things that need to be out all the time, such as the kettle or knife block. It also keeps these things safely out of reach of children.

Tiles: Strong horizontal lines play their part throughout this kitchen tricking the eye into thinking it is bigger than it really is. The tiles run round all three sides, mirroring the lines of the worktop and are topped by a narrow band in a strong contrasting color. The shelving and the blind also play on this theme of horizontal lines emphasizing the width of the room again and again.

Space invader

Does going for maximum storage mean you have to sacrifice style? Not a bit of it if you choose the right colors and clean lines.

Cabinets: If all your base-cabinet space is taken up with appliances the only way forward is to fill the walls with storage. Repetition is calming and easy on the eye and this has been used to great effect with this system of box storage on the wall. Arranged as a checkerboard of open shelving and closed cabinets it provides a pleasing feature and a place to stash the more unsightly kitchen essentials.

Backsplash: Rather than conventional tiles some cheap and cheerful tongue and groove panelling has been used to make a backsplash. Painted in a gloss or eggshell finish it is waterproof and wipes clean. The strong vertical lines of the panelling help the proportions of the space.

Skylight: If there's an opportunity to add extra light into a room pounce on it. A skylight gives wonderful overall daylight and just needs the addition of halogen spotlights for night-time. These will give a crisp white light that's as refreshing as natural daylight.

Dining: Although it's little more than a galley it has been possible to build a little eating area in on the left-hand side with just enough room for two people to share a cosy breakfast. The work surface that forms the breakfast bar has been shaped so that it's a narrow ledge along the main part of the kitchen then kicks out to make full use of the corner at the end.

Perfect planning

A tiny bathroom might seem a hopeless cause when it comes to spacious living but show a splash of creativity and you can pull off a marvellous transformation.

Scale drawing: With such a small area to work in it is essential to plan your bathroom carefully. First, do a scale drawing of the room on graph paper, then draw the bathroom suite to scale and cut out each piece. Move the shapes around on the graph paper until you get a layout you like. Remember to take into account the position of windows and doors, and, most importantly, the plumbing. It's not impossible to change the position but it can be costly.

Vanity cabinet: A cabinet built around a sink provides useful space for toiletries, cleaning materials and even dirty laundry. The sleek lines of the cabinet also help conceal the muddled effect that results from having too many freestanding items in a tiny space. Although the cabinet will take up more floor space it helps lead the eye around the room and gives a more streamlined appearance.

Shower enclosure: Building a small tiled wall between the sink and bathtub gives visual interest but as the lines of paint and tiles are carried right around it doesn't overwhelm. Tiling the faucet end of the bathtub completely could turn this into a shower enclosure doing away with the need for a fussy shower curtain.

Color: Don't hold back – deep color can work wonders in small spaces, adding drama, warmth and character. Choose plain finishes rather than patterned to enhance the space and balance a strong shade with pale wood or lighter tiles.

Mirror image

Most Victorian and Edwardian houses have tiny bathrooms as the toilet would have been in an outhouse. But color and light can help make them appear less cramped.

Mirror: Fit one entire wall with mirror (it might seem a little 1980s but it works). You'll be surprised how effective it is at creating a sense of space. Mirrors are most effective when they are placed on a wall opposite a window as they'll catch and reflect every available bit of light and bounce it around the room.

Window: In a tiny space like this any window treatment will add to the clutter and cut down on precious light levels. Better by far to leave the window unadorned and to frost the glass to provide privacy. If you must have some sort of window treatment make it a neat roller blind in a color to match the wall for a barely-there effect.

Storage: One wall has been boxed in to provide storage behind the wooden façade and on the ledge at the top. The pipework for the bathroom also runs unobtrusively behind this false wall for a more stream-lined finish. The ledge drops down in the center to accommodate the sink without the need for a pedestal which would break up the floor area.

Sink: A shallow sink in a style more commonly seen in utility rooms has been fitted to keep the lines of the bathroom lean and minimal. The mirror on the wall has been drilled to allow the faucet to come straight out of the wall.

TIP
Heated pads are available which fix to the wall behind mirrors to keep them slightly warm and stop them steaming up.

A bigger splash

The secret of having a well-groomed bathroom is to stash away as many things as possible while still keeping them handy.

Towels: Think boutique hotel chic and install a smart chrome towel rail high on a wall just to one side of the end of the bathtub. It will keep freshly laundered towels right where you need them but stop them getting sprayed by the shower.

Sink: A sink doesn't need to be large so think small and recessed to maximize your standing space. Make sure that you use wall-mounted tumblers and racks where possible to keep the sides of a small sink clear. The area below the sink is normally wasted but it's the perfect spot for fitting in a slimline cabinet. If you choose a cabinet on legs it will help create a feeling of space as you will be able to see the floor continue under it.

Going up: Give prime position to a spring-loaded storage pole that holds accessories such as a mirror, shelves for shampoo and toiletries and rings for towels. You'll find similar cabinets on sale at bigger bathroom specialist stores.

Walls: Cool blue and shiny chrome accessories help to give the impression of space by enhancing and reflecting light, while neat mosaic tiles add to the contemporary look. Don't think you have to stick to small tiles in a small room. Large tiles can have a very streamlining and space-enhancing effect.

TIP
Choose a laundry bin on wheels and make easy work of getting dirty clothes to the washing machine.

Two into one

If your home has a downstairs toilet does it really need a separate one upstairs too? You might prefer to create a spacious bathing area that doesn't cramp your style.

Space: There's no denying it, having separate toilets eases the clamour for the bathroom in the mornings. But if you've already got a downstairs toilet, taking down the wall between the bathroom and toilet upstairs will give you masses more room and the opportunity to make a really luxurious space. You'll need the advice of a builder or structural engineer before tackling this type of job.

Suite: Planning the bathroom suite along one wall gives you the maximum free floor space – and the smaller your bathroom the more important this becomes. It also keeps all the water and waste pipework close together, which makes the plumbing easier and neater. White is the smart choice for a suite and the glossy surface will enhance the natural light levels of the room.

Color: Broad panels of tiles and color on the wall play on the room's height, drawing the eye up towards the ceiling. They also work to define the sink area, dividing the space visually without the need for a physical barrier.

Storage: Banks of simple galvanized shelves are ranked on the walls providing ample space for everyday toiletries. A freestanding caddy can be moved from sink to bathtub as needed. Cleaning materials and other items you want to hide away are stashed beneath the upholstered lid of a seat.

Luscious curves

When you plan a new bathroom take full advantage of the innovative suite designs now available. When you consider that the average bathroom is no bigger than a king-size bed you know it makes sense.

Bathtub: Fed up with wet, clinging shower curtains draping around the bathtub? If there's no room for a separate bathtub and shower cubicle, a shaped bathtub, with a shower screen to match its shape, is the natural choice. Wider at the shower end, it will give you all the comfort of a roomy shower cubicle without gobbling up all the floor space. The foot end of the bathtub is narrower to give plenty of room alongside for a sink and toilet.

Sink: A small cloakroom sink will save space but a full-size wall-hung sink is more comfortable to use. Having it semi-recessed into a reduced-depth built-in storage cabinet is a clever use of available space being much less bulky than a standard cabinet. And it does away with messy plumbing on display! The cabinet also conceals the loo cistern giving a clean and stylish line to that whole side of the bathroom.

Floor: Large tiles seem a bold choice but manage to make the floor area seem bigger as it's not broken up into lots of little areas. The sparkly-glass effect adds a little extra gloss and glamour to the scheme.

Space makers

If you have the luxury of refitting a bathroom and space is tight, go for one of the dedicated systems designed to save space. **Suite:** With each piece designed to tuck neatly into a corner this suite is the most effective on the market for a really tight space. It can even be used to squeeze an ensuite into the corner of a bedroom without cramping your style too much. Note how there is still plenty of room around the fittings for the usual accessories such as a bin and towel ring. The sink and toilet are good options for use in a downstairs cloakroom as having them on an angle in this way might just free up a little more elbow-room.

Shower: The bi-fold shower door opens inwards meaning you don't need masses of floor space to maneuver around it. Despite the miserly amount of space this suite needs, the shower is comfortably spacious – a sign of very good design.

Door: Having the ensuite door open out into the bedroom is another way to keep the size of the bathroom to the absolute minimum. No space for it to open outwards? Try fitting a pair of narrow doors that need less room to open into or a sliding door.

TIP
Big bathroom retailers now offer the same computer design service that you expect from kitchen companies. Go armed with a scale plan of your room and a clear idea of your budget.

Think big

Just because a space is small it doesn't mean your ideas have to be. Be bold and see how much you can fit into a tiny room.

Bath: There is no real right and wrong when it comes to planning space. If you have your heart set on a corner bath and nothing else is going to make it the bathroom of your dreams then go for it. Just be aware that you will be losing floor space. But what do you gain in return? A huge bathing and showering space that you can share with your nearest and dearest (very eco-friendly!).

Screen: Rather than going the traditional glass screen route, this room has been treated to a very special curved wall. Made from flexible plywood and tiled with waterproof adhesive and grout it makes an eye-catching feature and encloses the shower without dividing the room.

Sink: On the opposite side of the curved wall the sink is slotted in neatly. No storage opportunity has been missed and niches have been carved out of the stud wall to make space for toiletries. The sink itself is big and chunky and rests on a thick ledge, painted to look like stone.

Tiles: Tiny mosaic tiles have been used in broad swathes to avoid a bitty, cluttered effect. The wide blue stripe runs right around the room to pull the different areas together and makes the room appear bigger.

Window: This room is not overlooked so there is no need for a window treatment which would simply clutter the room and get soaked by the shower. The glass in the bathroom door has been frosted for privacy.

All square

At a scant 6 ½ x 6 ½', bathrooms don't come much smaller than this one, but it's a pleasure to use and fulfils its family bathroom function perfectly.

Suite: A plain and simple budget suite from a big hardware store was the starting point for this room and it has been lined up along one wall for an orderly feel. The room itself is only about 12" longer than the bath so the gap was filled with water-proof plywood on a frame of wooden battens to make a shelf at the end of the bath.

Storage: The side of the bath and the ledge at the end have been tiled to match the wall, but not before a concealed cabinet was created in the end of the bath panel. This gives access to the space under the bath and makes a great place to stash toilet paper rolls and cleaning materials. On the wall hang simple MDF (medium density fiberglass) cubes, made from off-cuts and painted to match the walls. Toiletries and ornamental bits and pieces find a place here.

Door: In period houses doors are hung to open into the middle of a bathroom or bedroom to provide extra privacy when they are ajar, so this one originally opened to the right. Re-hanging it to open flat against the wall on the left made the space much more usable.

Window: A neat made-to-measure Roman blind hangs at the window, but rather than raise and lower the blind every time the bathroom is used the lower pane of the sash has been re-glazed with frosted glass.

Box it up

Learn how to turn problems to your advantage and you're well on the way to a space-friendly home.

Wall: In this bathroom the plumbing for the suite had to run all along one wall. To box it in and disguise it a false wall was built, but rather than accept losing 6" off the room, this was used as an opportunity to build an interesting feature and some useful storage. The wall was stopped at around 4' high so it forms a ledge running the length of the room. Fully tiled it is a waterproof area for toiletries and leafy green plants.

Tiles: Tiling a bathroom from top to toe is very space enhancing. If you don't want to go that far (if you've chosen very expensive tiles, for instance) a similar effect can be had by tiling as far as you want to then painting the remaining wall area in exactly the same color for continuity. Using micro-tiles all in one shade adds a little welcome texture to an otherwise totally plain room.

Faucets: Choose a bath with a central waste and position the faucets in the middle of the wall to free up each end (this was easy here as the stud wall was already planned to conceal the plumbing). That way two can bathe comfortably together and no one gets the faucet end!

Sit and sleep

Living rooms extend their welcome when they can be easily transformed into bedrooms for occasional overnight guests.

Sofa bed: A sofa bed is the essential buy for an instant extra bedroom. You'll want one that's as good for sleeping on as it is for snuggling on, so expect to pay around $1000. Look for a sprung mattress and a steel frame. Sit on it to check that the frame doesn't dig into the back of your legs, then open it out and lie on it. Remember, a sofa will give a little over time so don't be put off if it feels firm to start with.

Screen: A screen is a great asset when you are trying to make one room do two jobs. Make one from four pieces of ply or MDF (medium density fiberglass) hinged together. By day it will hide bedding tucked into a corner or alcove, by night it converts quickly to a stylish hanging space with the addition of a wooden batten slipped through a pair of drilled holes.

Tables: A low table works hard day and night as a coffee table, a bedside table and a temporary dressing table.

Lighting: Mood lighting helps the room switch purpose from sitting to sleeping. Consider low-level lamps and candles as well as overhead lighting. A pair of standard lamps either side of the sofa cast just the right light for reading whether by day or just as you snuggle down for the night.

Color: Calming blues and naturals are a good color combination, helping the transition from light, fresh, living space to restful bedroom.

Heads you win

Bedrooms for children and teenagers will offer you one of the biggest storage challenges ever. The trick is to make the storage arrangements stylish and fun so they actually get used and to create double-purpose furniture that really earns its keep!

Headboard: Find someone who's handy with a saw and get them to rustle up a useful bed head that doubles neatly as a huge bedside table. Made from ¼"-thick MDF (medium density fiberglass) it provides heaps of storage for books, CDs, a CD player and other essential bits and pieces. If you make one side panel removable (perhaps secured with magnetic catches) it will make another large storage area inside the base of the headboard.

Power: With a power socket fitted to the wall behind the headboard and a couple of holes drilled through to accommodate cables, the wires for a music system and bedside light can be tucked neatly and safely out of the way.

Bed: Choose a simple low-level divan for a child's room. In a small space low furniture is more space enhancing and easier for kids to use. Pile it up with cushions during the daytime to encourage them to lounge around listening to music with their friends in here rather than occupying your living room!

TIP
For an even more space-enhancing effect paint the headboard in the same color as the wall and it will virtually disappear into the background.

Best of both worlds

Two sets of furniture? Who needs it when you can find pieces that will live just as happily indoors or out saving you the problem of finding a winter storage place for garden tables and chairs.

Materials: The secret to buying furniture that will work just as well indoors or out is in the materials that you choose. It's probably easiest to look for garden furniture that fits into your indoor schemes so that you can be sure that the pieces you choose will stand up to the weather without having to be rushed indoors every time you see a cloud. Painted or lacquered metals, woven willow, resin and hardwoods are all available so you'll be able to find something that suits whatever your style.

Shape: Bistro-style furniture that has a holiday café feel about it is ideal for use in a kitchen or informal dining area. French-style is hot news too at the moment and curly metalwork chairs with pierced seats and matching tabletops look a treat used in the house or out on the patio.

Stacking: Folding or stacking furniture is especially good as extra chairs can be tucked away into a cupboard or hung from hooks on the wall when they are not needed.

Care: Furniture that's expected to spend at least part of its life outside in all weathers needs a little special care to keep its good looks. Wooden furniture should be oiled annually, paint and lacquer should be wiped down with mild detergent and dried. Any rust patches or flaking paint should be treated immediately to prevent long-term damage.

TIP

A round table with a pedestal base is the most space efficient giving you plenty of surface area without anyone having to sit by a leg.

Studio bliss

What teenagers want is a sense of independence and that means giving them somewhere they can sleep, chill out and be with their friends – so how does that fit into the average bedroom?

Platform: A raised bed is one way to make extra space but why not take it to the absolute limit and build a platform for sleeping? It doesn't need a huge amount of headroom if you keep the bed arrangements low (a futon mattress and duvet is ideal) and leaves the floor below free for other uses. This bed is built on a metal frame made from scaffolding poles. The same poles have been used to construct a spiky staircase for access to the platform. Sprayed silver it looks more like a piece of modern sculpture.

Seating: A couple of small armchairs and a beanbag or two will give plenty of room for lounging around listening to music. Removable washable covers are always a good idea in this sort of room. Another idea would be inflatable furniture that simply rolls up and tucks into a drawer when not in use.

Washing: Ease the squeeze on the bathroom by tucking a small hand sink into a corner which will do perfect duty for a quick wash or teeth cleaning. Add a small fridge for drinks and conceal with a trendy screen and you might even forget you've got kids …

Lighting: Good lighting is essential in a small space like this if it is not to look cluttered. A roof light is a huge advantage but a row of halogen spotlights in the ceiling would give a similar clean white light. Make sure the space under the platform is also adequately lit – dimmers make it easy to change the mood.

Home office

Whether you work from home or simply want somewhere organized for the kids to do their homework, the chances are your office space has to be squeezed into a corner of another room. Here's how to make it work.

Desk: Choose a desk that will sit neatly along one wall and that has a second surface area that wheels around with a smooth move to fit around a corner and give you plenty of workspace.

Technology: The latest computers are compact and so stylish you won't mind having them on display. The new iMacs do away with the big box that held the hard drive and they're even more space efficient if you pop them on a monitor stand to free up the desk area. For even more space efficiency you could choose one of the new laptops with a large screen which will then just slip into a drawer when the working day is over.

Storage: Use the wall for racks and baskets to take paperwork and stationery. Choose a theme, say chrome or aluminum, and stick to it to give the area a sleek designer look. The less often you use something the higher up the wall it can go leaving lower-level space for everyday essentials.

Filing: A small filing cabinet on wheels can be kept close by while you work then simply rolled out of the way below the desk at knock-off time. Don't let paperwork expand into two or three cabinets when one will do. Be ruthless about what you keep – and what you print out. It's much better (and cheaper) to back things up onto CD or floppy disk than print and file endless sheets of paper.

Be my guest

A guest room is all the more welcoming if it has a few extra home comforts and all the more useful if it can step up to the mark as a temporary dormitory for teenagers.

Seating: If visitors want to chill out at any point without getting under your feet a futon is a cheap and cheerful way to provide some seating in the spare room where they can relax, read or put on make-up. Small and simple, it's often possible to squeeze this type of sofa in where a chunkier traditional model just wouldn't fit. Futons are also available in single, chair-size models for the tightest of spaces.

Beds: A room with two single beds is more flexible than a room with a double bed, after all, not all of your visitors will be couples. A double futon would turn this room into a little dormitory for very young children at big family events such as holidays or weddings.

Colors: A very basic two-color scheme leaves the room feeling clear, clean and fresh. The blue tones of the futon and the fresh leafy green on the wall have been repeated on the bedlinen, cushions and the throw for an easy-on-the-eye look while the floorboards have simply been sanded back to pale pine and varnished.

Shelving: Plain pine shelving complements the stripped floor and fills an otherwise unused space above the head of the bed doing away with the need for a bedside table which would cramp the futon.

Rise and fall

The run of cabinets in this room does not one, not two but three jobs! That's got to be great value in anyone's book.

Storage: This room doubles as a sitting and dining area piling on extra storage space for china and glass as well as the usual books and videos. Long and low, the cabinets running all along one side of this living/dining room rise to the occasion providing all the space you could possibly wish for. The doors are kept sleek with push catches rather than handles that protrude and catch on anything that passes.

Display: The long ledge formed by the top of the cabinets makes a perfect display area. Repetition is a good trick to use if you want impact without a cluttered effect. A collection of different flowering plants would look jungly and messy but a series of single exotic leaves arranged in matching metal vases suggests calm and order – simply beautiful!

Heating: Hidden behind the slatted area of the storage system is the room's radiator. Normally an eyesore and a hassle to work around, this way it is tucked out of sight while the open slats allow the heat to circulate freely and efficiently.

Seating: While the tan leather sofas do a great job for lounging, extra seating has been built into the run of storage by dropping the level and adding a couple of cushions covered in a natural calico to team with the scheme. If extra people are expected for dinner the table can be moved across to the built-in seat rather than having to find extra chairs.

Lofty looks

Open-plan loft-style living looks lovely on paper, but what really happens when your kitchen is also your dining room and study?

Color: There is a temptation in multi-purpose spaces to use color to define different areas but that can create a cramped and muddled look. It's much nicer to devise a color scheme that works for all the room's uses and decorate the space as one.

Furniture: One really clever piece of furniture makes this space completely functional for its three uses. A table has been designed with a laminated top and lockable wheels on the legs. By day it wheels into place over the fridge and freezer in the kitchen area to provide a worktop area but at the drop of a hat it slides out to become a desk or, in the evening, a dining table with plenty of room for entertaining friends. Open slatted chairs have a lightweight look and stack together when not in use.

Window: Neat made-to-measure blinds sit inside the window recess giving a clean line. A fabric to match the color of the walls was chosen for an uninterrupted block of color when the blinds are drawn at night.

Study: In a tiny space a laptop replaces a traditional desktop computer and is tucked into a spare kitchen drawer when not in use. With the addition of a cordless phone all this office space needs is a small filing cabinet on wheels that can be trundled off to use as a coffee table in the evening.

Sew easy

It can save you huge amounts of money on soft furnishings if you are handy with a sewing machine but first you need somewhere convenient to work.

Find space: There are few homes that have the luxury of a room that can be given over to sewing so start by thinking small. What you need to find is a decent alcove in a room that's currently not over-used that you can use to create a mini-workroom with the sewing machine permanently set up and ready to go. A sewing room can easily double up with a bedroom, study or dining room.

Sort it: Once you've identified your space you need to be rigorous in exploiting every single inch. Rather than try to squeeze a table in, put a shelf across at work-table height so it fills the full width and depth of the alcove. Fill out the wall above with small shelves, a peg rail or perhaps a pin board so that your sewing kit can have a permanent home where it's easily accessible.

Add a small stool that will tuck neatly away under the bench. A stack of pretty boxes would give you heaps of storage for patterns, ribbons, trimmings and fabric remnants.

Hide away: You could conceal your alcove with a simple curtain with eyelet heading slipped onto a wire. Much neater, however, is a system of sliding panels. Wooden artist's stretchers covered with canvas make perfect doors. Some art shops will make them to measure using your own fabric. Screw castors to the base and cup hooks into the top, then hook over a length of tension wire so the doors can slide to one side.

Bonus bedroom

With a little imagination and a whole load of planning even a modestly-proportioned room can be made to give up enough space to fit in an office.

Bed: If a room is for regular use a sofa bed is unlikely to be comfortable and durable enough. Similarly, if two people are to sleep here a standard double bed is essential for a good night's rest. So, a standard bed it has to be but you can do away with big bulky headboards and if you choose a low-level platform bed you will help the proportions enormously.

Desk: There's no spare floor space in this room. It measures just 11 x 9' but by day no one needs to get around the bed so the space at the foot is given over to two small folding tables which simply flip up into place when they're needed. A stylish chair doubles up for both bedroom and study purposes.

Storage: Not one square inch is wasted and the full height of the room is exploited with shelving that is deep enough to hold computer equipment and box files. As this is not just an office but a relaxing space too, care has been taken with the shelving to make it as attractive as possible. Split bamboo has been tacked and glued to the edge of each shelf giving a contemporary finish.

Hide it: If you wouldn't be able to relax faced with a whole wall of office supplies then a simple row of white roller blinds fixed to the ceiling would be the answer. Pull them down in front of the shelves at night to hide everything in an instant.

To dine for

It's asking a lot for a space to switch from hard-working kitchen to relaxing entertaining area but it can be done with some clever design tricks.

Blinds: The most innovative thing about this room is the way roller blinds have been used as a disguise for worktop clutter. As the meal comes together and guests gather at the table, the blinds, mounted on the ceiling, are simply pulled down to conceal all the cooking utensils, pots and pans that have been used while cooking. Even the sink and microwave disappear behind the screening effect of the blinds.

Units: The wall units in this room have been chosen for their mix of solid and glass doors. Each provides plenty of space for storage but the prettiest items are reserved to go on display in the glass-fronted units. If you have a lot of gadgets and kitchenware, planning in one or two full-height stacks of drawers in place of a couple of base

cabinets is a good move and will let you work more efficiently with everything stored neatly and close to hand.

Furniture: A smart bistro-style table and chairs have been chosen for their ability to switch from functional family meals to café-style entertaining with the addition of a floor-length drape of rose pink fabric. The table folds so it can be stashed out of the way if more space is needed while preparing food.

Plate rack: A gap above the sink has been filled with a plate rack which means china can go straight from the sink onto the rack to dry and doesn't need to take up cabinet space.

Garden room

In summer when life naturally spills outside be sure you're making the most of your garden.

Entertaining: Sociable summer evenings are the time to put on your biggest parties. There's no point in trying to squeeze extra people into a small dining room when your garden is the perfect space for entertaining. Drinks on the lawn, supper on the terrace – doesn't it sound inviting and stylish? You just need to be sure you've got what it takes to make everyone comfortable, and that means spending a little time – and some cash – on the right furniture and accessories.

Relaxing: A towel on the lawn just won't do as a sunbed if your garden is to be a wonderful outdoor room for the duration of the summer. Make sure everyone has a seat and that there is a mix of chairs and loungers. Folding furniture that tucks into the shed when the weather turns is ideal.

Furniture: A full-size table that seats at least six and extends to accommodate eight or even ten is ideal. If there's no room for everyone to be seated comfortably at the table do supper as a buffet and use the table to lay everything out for people to help themselves. Arrange loungers, deck chairs, even the kitchen chairs on the lawn and let everyone find their own place.

Lighting: Garlands of outdoor christmas lights will bring a magical twinkle to trees and bushes. Scatter tealights in glass jars among the flower beds and save a couple of large candles in lanterns for the far end of the garden to lead the eye right the way down.

Study this

Having a piece of furniture custom-built is the way forward if you are serious about making a small space perform two functions. This spare-room-cum-study got the full treatment.

Bed: Trying to fit a double bed, fitted wardrobes and a study area into a room that is roughly twice the size of the bed is quite a challenge but by building an all-in-one piece of furniture to fit the room it has been achieved – and with some style! The bed is positioned against the wall and framed on the other side by a full-length cabinet. Small niches perform the function of a bedside table, holding books, a clock and drinks. Even more storage is built in under the bed frame and accessed via sliding doors. The overall effect is cosy and almost like being in a cabin on a liner.

Study: At the end of the bed the footboard goes right up to ceiling height forming a room divider. Off the back of this a desk and shelves have been built with split cane roller blinds to drop down and cover up all the box files and computer.

Radiator: Slender vertical radiators take up next to no space on the wall. In a royal blue powder-coating finish they repeat the strong blue vertical lines throughout the room, which helps give a welcome sense of height.

Across the divide

It is possible to create different areas for different purposes within one room without making life cramped. Here's how a living room and dining room can work together but still have their own identities.

Materials: It might seem like a tall order to divide one space into two without losing the overall feeling of space but it can be achieved. Glass bricks are the solution to the problem. They look fabulous with sunlight shining through them, come in a range of colors including blue, aqua, green and clear and have a real up-to-the-minute designer feel. You can buy them at hardware stores and create your own screen if you have a handy person around the house. Otherwise it's probably best to call in a professional to lay them.

Proportion: This is not the place for a solid wall of bricks. What you are aiming for is an impression of two rooms rather than a complete physical barrier. Instead opt for slender columns of blocks within an MDF (medium density fiberglass) frame, held in place with silicone sealant.

Color: Let the sparkle of the glass set the tone for a light-enhancing, glossy and pale color scheme. Laminate boards in pale limed oak or ash, or even a look-alike vinyl will bring a sheen to the floor which will bounce light up and around the whole room. Barely-there sugared almond shades will provide a pretty touch. Allow one shade extra prominence at each end of the room, and both living and dining areas will be clearly defined within the overall color scheme.

Clear winner

The height of bedroom luxury is to have a separate dressing area where you can store shoes, bags and accessories and have your dressing table set up with good clear lighting.

Planning: Work out the smallest space you need for your dressing area then draw your bedroom onto graph paper. Cut out pieces of paper to scale to represent your furniture and arrange them on the paper to see how you might create the space you need. In a long narrow room consider moving the bed towards the center of the room so the dressing area is at one end behind the head of the bed.

Divide: A sheet of clear Perspex makes a great screen if you add a design in etching spray, which will give privacy if your bedroom is overlooked but allow light to flow through. Mask off a pattern (geometrics are simple and stylish) with tape and apply a couple of coats of etching spray.

Hanging: To hang the screen, drill small holes 2" from the top and screw corresponding eye screws into the ceiling (making sure they are screwed into a joist and not just the plaster board of the ceiling). Hang the screen from the hooks with fine chain.

TIP
Etching spray is available in white or pastel colors if you want to tone the screen with your room's color scheme.

Use every inch

If there is a place for everything – and things get put in their place – space will cease to be an issue. What it takes is some full-on planning.

Divider: Being able to divide one space into two can be a real advantage if you do it the right way. A simple screen would do the job but a wheeled shelving unit works so much harder providing bags of storage space that can be accessed from both sides. And when you need the space back as one again it simply turns sideways to stand against the wall.

Open or closed?: Tidy types can afford to choose open storage and show off their treasures. Messy monsters are better with closed cabinets and hideaway storage bins.

Wheels: Whatever storage you choose, an option on wheels is always a winner. Your space will be so much more flexible if you

can easily slide the room divider, the coffee table or even the sofa aside to make way for a party, a games evening or even a workout in front of that exercise video!

CDs: They might only be little but they can add to the clutter in a room if you haven't got a designated storage area. Wall racks are a great idea – they keep the CDs off the coffee table but give you instant access to your music.

Coffee tables: Don't miss a single opportunity to build more storage into a room. A coffee table with shelves and drawers is the ideal place for magazines, boxes of CDs, books and even paperwork if it's filed in stylish boxes. A little side table with a removable lid that reveals yet more storage space could be home to bedlinen for a sofa bed or even the bar cabinet!

TIP
If you are building a lot of storage into a scheme think carefully about the materials you use. Aim for a seamless finish by choosing furniture in one wood shade.

Center point

The way that you screen or divide up a room can make a big difference.

Space: Defining living areas with full- or half-height screens, especially ones that include storage, will create a sense of order. Half-height dividing walls are particularly useful tools as they let the eye travel uninterrupted while hiding a multitude of sins behind them. In this room the addition of an RSJ (reinforced steel joist) has allowed a slot to be cut out of the wall creating a fascinating feature and linking two spaces successfully while keeping them well defined.

Color: Using complementary colors or different tones of one color in adjoining spaces creates a natural link between them. Keep the shades very similar and it will create a real sense of space. Use the palest colors at the far end of the room and it will appear to push the wall away, making the room seem bigger than ever.

Go vertical: Take every opportunity to build in a little extra storage – especially if it delivers an interesting shot of style into the bargain. This expanding pole fits between floor and ceiling and is designed to hold plant pots but makes a great stashing point for magazines or even for fruit and veg in the kitchen.

TIP
Plant pots that stick to the window on suckers keep herbs handy but clear of the worktop.

Two into one

One space or two? – the choice is yours.

Modern style: Open-plan living is not for everyone and not for every occasion. If you have adjoining living and dining rooms there may be times when you want them opened out together for large family gatherings and other times when you'd prefer to feel cosily closed in. Taking a wall down between the spaces gives you the two-in-one space while adding glass-paned doors gives you the option to divide the spaces back up again.

Blinds: The advantages of the large glass doors are clear. They split the space but allow a view through to the next room and the garden beyond. The disadvantage is the space they need to open fully – space that can't be occupied by furniture if the doors are to be functional at all times. Instead, hanging vertical blinds across the opening gives you the flexibility to ring the changes with the space, but without the need for extra room to open and close them. Similar style blinds are used in the room beyond but in a paler color for its receding properties.

Floor: If you can't (or don't want to) take the same flooring material throughout areas of your home you can achieve a similar space-enhancing effect by choosing materials in similar tones. In this dining room slate-effect laminate tiles lead out onto a patio of grey stone-effect slabs blurring the line between inside and out.

Made for sharing

When you're a kid all you want is a space to call your own. Here's how to please everyone when there's not enough rooms to go round.

Space: Two sometimes have to go into one when it comes to bedrooms. If you're feeling generous you might have given up the largest bedroom to the kids who have to share but overall space isn't everything, it's personal space that counts and it's time to come up with a clever way to divide up the room.

Storage: The starting point in this room is a bank of waist-high shelving. Accessible from both sides it gives bags of space for toys, games and shoes and goes a long way in defining the space occupied by each child. Roller blinds fitted to the front of each cubby-hole hide the inevitable clutter from sight.

Blinds: Fitting long roller-blinds in a row along the ceiling above the central storage is the masterstroke that makes this room work as two. Each child can choose their own color scheme with central blinds chosen to team or contrast with each side. They can be left plain or personalized with braids, decorative pulls or shaped bottom-edges. Fitted so they pull down to meet the storage bank they will effectively split the room to give privacy if someone has to go to bed early or wants to read or do homework. Blackout fabrics are also available if you have a child that wakes when the sun rises in summer.

TIP
Matching blinds can also be made to fit skylight windows for a completely coordinated look.

Glass distinction

If you have the luxury of a large bedroom you might be able to accommodate an en suite to ease the squeeze on the family bathroom.

Walls: In an en suite there is slightly less emphasis on privacy than there is with a family bathroom where guests would find this sort of exposure rather intimidating! Glass bricks make a terrific alternative to a solid stud wall if you are carving up a room and allow light to stream through uninterrupted. This room is admittedly of generous proportions and the en suite enjoys the luxury of a roll-top bath, but even a modestly-sized bedroom could provide enough space for a shower enclosure, toilet and sink in a corner and using glass as the dividing material will reduce its impact on the space.

Furniture: Continue the glass theme with the furniture to provide useful surfaces that have a barely-there effect. This concentration of glass and mirror will bring welcome light and sparkle to the room, which are wonderfully space-enhancing. Delicate curly wrought iron gives an airier feel than heavy wood or laminate would offer.

Floor: In keeping with the light, bright theme, the original floorboards have been scrubbed along the grain with a wire brush then treated with coats of white wax for a limed finish. The wax will wear off the edges and high points of the boards with use, giving a mellow, worn effect.

A fresh start

Storage and de-cluttering are mantras of 21st-century living – for a reason. A good old-fashioned clear out will make your home feel instantly bigger.

Sort it: Work through your home one room at a time being firm with yourself about what is worth keeping and which things you can wave goodbye to. Dispose of anything that has been broken for 12 months or longer or that has exceeded its use-by date. Don't attempt to do the whole house at once or you will just feel as if it is an impossible job. One room a month will soon have the place looking ship-shape.

Furniture: Anything broken that you haven't bothered to restore, anything that's surplus to your needs and anything that you don't really like but hang onto for sentimental reasons are all candidates for the next trip to the tip.

Box clever: If you moved house over a year ago and still have boxes unopened in the loft or garage you can be fairly sure that you don't need (or want) the contents. Harden your heart and free your space – it can all be binned or recycled and give you the head and house space for lovely new things that you will appreciate.

Disposal: Once you've identified the things that need to go, sort them out into piles: one for the charity shop, one for the recycling center and one for the trash.

TIP
Once you've organized your possessions keep them that way. Clutter creeps up little by little and eats into your personal space – if you let it...

Wall to wall

When you're struggling to make things fit, taking a whole slice off the side of your bedroom might not seem the best way forward, but fitted storage is absolutely the best option for using every square inch.

Cabinets: Made to measure cabinets built to fit your space are the ultimate and will ensure you use all the space available. They are especially useful in rooms with awkward shapes or sloping ceilings and can be tailor-made to any shape and with any combination of storage inside. A cheaper option that you can take with you if you move is to fit modular cabinets that you buy flat-packed and which simply bolt together to make an uninterrupted run of cabinets.

Doors: Mirror doors were the space-enhancing choice of the 1970s but who wants to catch sight of themselves getting out of bed after a heavy night? A more modern choice is painted frames inset with either plain or frosted glass. If your cabinets tend towards messy, frosted glass is a kinder option and will conceal the contents. Avoid fussy details like lots of little panes of glass and keep to long, lean and simple lines.

Shelves and rails: Make sure you include a good mix of shelf space and hanging rails. Before you make your choice take an inventory of the type of things you are likely to store in your wardrobe. There is no point in having hanging space to take full-length dresses if you live in jeans and t-shirts. One thing that everyone underestimates is the amount of space taken up by shoes. You might not be Imelda Marcos but chances are you still have at least half a dozen pairs of shoes/sandals/sneakers tossed to the bottom of your wardrobe. Shoe racks might not sound glamorous but they are a space-enhancing addition, will help keep your footwear in good shape and if you can make room for them you should.

The bigger picture

Small architectural alterations can work miracles, changing the appearance of a room and needn't cost the earth.

Window: Increasing the size of a window, or even turning it into floor-to-ceiling doors, is a relatively inexpensive alteration and can make an enormous difference, especially if you look out onto a garden. These sliding doors have a simple frame and huge glass panes and allow an uninterrupted view down the entire length of the garden even when shut. The light levels soar because of the expanse of glass lifting the atmosphere and giving a fresh, outdoor feel to the room.

Decoration: If you go down this route, repeat the colors that you have used decoratively inside on garden furniture and the potted plants outside. Consider using the same, or similar, flooring throughout. It will blur the boundaries between indoors and outside and make the space seem endless. A natural theme is ideal in this situation with chunky, woven seagrass furniture, wooden flooring and lots of leafy greens.

Curtains: With windows this big you'll be sure to need some sort of window treatment to provide privacy in the evenings when the lights are on. If you choose curtains make sure the pole extends at least 6" either side of the window so that the fabric can be pulled right back off the glass during the day to maximize the light and the view.

TIP
Provide extra seating with huge, natural, woven floor-cushions which look just as much at home inside or out.

Hang it all

There are times when every home is bulging at the seams with extra visitors and storage suddenly takes on a whole new importance. Some people are at ease living out of a suitcase and will happily adopt a slightly wrinkled appearance. Others, however, prefer a more orderly lifestyle and will thank you for providing somewhere to hang their clothes.

Hanging space: A dress rail is the modern way to accommodate this need for extra storage space and is a versatile piece of kit. Choose one that is height adjustable if you have sloping ceilings and it will slide neatly into an otherwise unused space under the eaves. Look out for models with a shelf at the bottom to take shoes and bags, and choose light-reflecting chrome for a sense of open airiness.

Kids' rooms: A dress rail isn't just for Christmas but makes itself useful even when the visitors have gone home. In kids' rooms, which tend to be the smaller bedrooms, it is far less bulky than a traditional wooden wardrobe.

Cover up: If you are bothered by the idea of dust it can simply tuck behind a curtain or have a neat calico cover run up to slip over the top.

Laundry day: A dress rail is a great accessory when it comes to tackling a pile of ironing. With this at your side everything can go straight onto hangers and onto the rail ready to be transferred neatly into the wardrobes. And at the end of the day it packs flat to slip into a cabinet until it's needed again.

Up the wall

A utility room is a highly practical addition to a home and worked to the full it will take a huge amount of pressure off the kitchen.

Peg rail: Shopping bags, hats, dog leads – the odds and ends that can be stored on a peg rail are almost endless. Buy them ready-made or rustle up your own using a length of batten and some wooden doorknobs or coat hooks. This should be the resting place for all those essential but less-than-lovely things that every home has and that usually clutter a kitchen or under-stairs cabinet.

Ironing: The number one space-saving solution for an ironing board is to have it built into a drawer cabinet in the kitchen. Failing that, get it off the floor and onto hooks on the wall and buy a special rack for your iron to hang alongside. These are quite widely available from department stores and homeware catalogs, and as well as getting your iron out of the way they have cord storage built in which helps prolong the life of the iron.

Appliances: In a small space keep things in proportion by opting for slimline appliances that will save you a few inches of valuable floor space. The capacity is obviously reduced along with the size but if a dishwasher and dryer are essentials to you, rather than luxuries, this is the way to fit them in.

Airer: Pretty as well as practical, an airer fixed to the ceiling on a pulley system will keep drying laundry out of dirt's way.

Dreams come true

Lost your bed under a pile of clothes? Reclaim your space and make the most of it with a few neat ideas.

Shelving: Freestanding cabinets with voile or calico covers in white or cream are readily available and bring instant order to a muddled bedroom. Stash all your odds and ends such as make-up, hair accessories, jewelery and undies in pretty coordinating boxes and stack them on the shelves and see just how much clutter you can bust!

Hang it: Plastic or canvas cabinets normally destined to be shut inside a wardrobe can be just as useful hanging from a high pole or hooks in the ceiling. You are more likely to use this type of storage – and keep it tidy – if it is instantly accessible rather than if it is hidden out of sight inside a cabinet.

Valance: If the very word valance conjures up flouncy images of ruffled dust-catchers then stop right there. A neat box-pleated valance will tidy up the base of your bed and with the addition of a few pockets stitched on gives you some great hidey-holes for shoes, books, newspapers – in fact all that junk that's usually on the bedside table or floor.

Bedside table: Actually, a table is by no means enough when you're trying to maximize space. What's needed is something with at least one drawer and a shelf and if you can find something with one, two or three cabinets or drawers you're onto a winner.

TIP
Plain pale colors are the most space enhancing. Allow yourself a little pattern on the bed covers to give the eye a treat.

Stow-aways

An alcove in a bedroom is the best feature you could wish for when it comes to storage in a kid's room.

Shelves: Filled with shelving (make it chunky for a modern look) an alcove will eat up books, videos, games and toys. There's something satisfying about things organized into neat stacks and it just needs a few pretty things carefully displayed to make an attractive corner. Keep breakables and more precious things on the top shelf out of everyday reach.

Boxes: Slot a couple of boxes on wheels underneath the bottom shelf to take toys that won't stack. If you're a do-it-yourself veteran make them to fit the space exactly using 3 ½" MDF (medium density fiberglass) and add castors to the bottom. Not so handy? Buy plastic storage crates. If they come with lids so much the better as they'll make great little tables for play when they slide out into the room.

Color scheme: Crisp apple green tempered with plenty of white gives this room a wide-open feel. Keeping the shelving and skirting white builds strong horizontal lines into the color scheme which helps make a narrow or cramped space seem to grow in width. To enhance this effect a wide white border has been painted right around the room at picture-rail height. This leads the eye up drawing attention to the height of the room as well.

TIP
To give this chunky look to existing shelving simply glue and screw lengths of battening along the front edge flush with the top surface. Fill the screw holes, sand and paint.

Sleek lines

Do you wonder how some people manage to live in more minimal style? There's no big secret – they've come to grips with storage.

Wall cabinets: While we can all head for the nearest superstore and stock up on ready-made cabinets at budget prices sometimes it does pay to invest a little extra and have storage custom-made – that way you get exactly the right proportion of shelves and cabinets in sizes to suit the things you need to store. Here a whole bank of recesses and cabinets has been created with areas for display, shelves of just the right size for videos, books and files and neat boxy cabinets for the things that don't merit being on show. Not an inch is wasted and the effect is of calm order rather than cluttered muddle. One true sign of a well organized home is the ability to leave one or two shelves completely empty!

Cabinets: The long, low run of cabinets is a modern take on the traditional sideboard. It provides bags of storage for toys and paperwork and is also home to the family's best china and glasses freeing up handy space in the kitchen. Low furniture like this is easier on the eye in a small space than taller pieces.

Color: Although the cabinet doors are picked out in trendy bright shades the effect is softened by the solid beech top which tones well with the creamy shade of the wall and recedes into the background.

TIP

A display area should be just that – for display – not a dumping ground for newspapers, mail and dirty cups. Choose your items carefully and remember that less is more.

Box clever

Even if you have a dining room chances are it's smaller than you would like so how do you make the most of it?

Storage: The modern dining room often has to double as playroom or study – that is if you have a dedicated dining room at all. More often, dining is done in the kitchen making every inch even more precious. A buffet or sideboard is out of the question in this case and some neat alternatives need to be found. Wall-mounted MDF (medium density fiberglass) boxes in various sizes and shapes make a striking feature on the wall as well as adding valuable extra storage space without taking up a single inch of floor – neat!

Chairs: Have the bare minimum of standard chairs to cater for your everyday needs but keep a stash of folding or stacking chairs tucked away so that more people can be seated at a moment's notice.

Table: So, you've got your folding chairs ready to spring into action when there's a big family supper but how do you make the table stretch? Easy! A large sheet of MDF or plywood laid over the top will give you a bigger surface and will rest safely in place. Cover the lot with a lavish white cloth (a sheet will do nicely), pile on the candles and smart tableware and dazzle 'em!

Window: No room here for fussy drapes and swags, and besides, they are right out of fashion just now. Instead opt for the sleek alternative of a Roman blind. Vertical stripes will make the window seem tall and elegant and this type of blind uses the scant minimum of fabric so you can push the boat out with something a bit special.

A niche market

When you're starting a room from scratch the opportunity is there to build in some stylish storage that will add an interesting feature to a plain space and make your home more streamlined and efficient.

Niches: A stud wall has been put up in this space to divide one large room into two more usable smaller ones. Rather than just build a plain wall, niches of varying sizes and shapes have been incorporated at different heights to display favorite things. With a narrow architrave around each one the vases and ceramics on show are framed, almost like pictures.

Bookcase: A narrow strip of wall might not seem to show too much promise for a nifty space-saving idea but shelved from top to bottom it is now home to the family's collection of books. This is a great example of stealing a little overlooked space back and putting it to good use.

Mirror: Rather than fill the entire wall with books, a central panel has been left open and the back of the recess filled with a mirror. Mirror is a classic space-enhancing tool, giving you a longer view and reflecting lots of light into and around a room. Cleverly, this mirror has a small picture hung on it at head height so that when you look at it your own reflection is masked, tricking you into thinking you really are seeing beyond into another room.

TIP
Take paneling on a wall right down to floor level without skirting board which would break up the long lines that enhance the height of the room.

Tight corner

If you feel as if every corner of your home is jam-packed take a fresh look. Corners are exactly where you might find that extra little space that will turn a room from tip to tidy.

Space: If your home is on the cramped side your first priority is to be realistic. A wide-screen, surround-sound TV system is probably not for you, no matter how much the kids plead. If you scale things down and keep them in proportion you'll find room for all your essentials – and a few luxuries too.

Storage: Retailers know how much it's possible to cram into an unused corner without impinging on the general feeling of space in a room. That's why furniture stores are jam-packed with TV stands, display cabinets and wall cabinets designed to fit fair and square into a corner. Buying ready-made is fine but go one step further and design your own piece to suit your own personal needs and the effect will be even better. In this room a built-in cabinet has been created across one corner and neatly incorporates the TV, a cabinet, shelves and even drawers.

Fireplace: The old 1930s fireplace has been ripped out and replaced with a decorative steel fire surround that sits completely flush with the wall taking up next to no space.

Color: It's big color contrasts that appear to break up and restrict a space. Painting the paneling, the wall and the built-in storage the same pretty shade of pale lavender makes one seamless wall of color.

Score with doors

Why is it there always seems to be a door in the way when you want to move the furniture around? Take control and make the space around the door one of your room's biggest assets.

Storage: If there's one thing this room has in abundance it's storage. But because it has been built as slim shelving on an otherwise poorly used wall it barely makes an impact on the available space in the room. Even the area above the door has been brought into play by taking the shelving up and over the frame. Built-in features such as wall-lights have been accommodated by designing large 'boxes' around them so they appear to be on display along with pictures, ceramics and a rather grand clock.

Flooring: Dark wooden flooring is a powerful feature in a compact home but using it throughout helps lead the eye from one room to the next giving a sense of continuity. The central area of each room has been highlighted with a colorful rug that keeps the wood from overwhelming the cottage garden colors of the walls.

Doors: Large double doors are an indulgent feature but mean that the ground floor of this home seems to flow together as one space. When privacy or quiet is called for they can be shut to enclose each room. Even when closed, large panels of glass in each door allow a view into the room beyond and let light filter through.

Acres of space

Sometimes a space just seems so awkward it's hard to know what to do with it, but chances are that, with a little careful planning, it will make a nifty storage area.

Space: Don't rule out the potential of any area as somewhere to stash stuff away. At first sight this under-stair area looked like a hopeless case with its chimney stack running below the stairs and making a large step in the wall.

Shelves: The solution to this tricky space was to fill the entire wall with shelves. Instead of letting them step out in line with the walls, the shelves were made deep and cut to fit around the step at the back leaving a long, straight edge at the front. This gives a vast and flexible area of storage with different depth shelves on each side to accommodate different sized belongings. The shelving stops at skirting height and the original plug sockets are still accessible below. Wires for the stereo system can simply be passed up the back of the shelves instead of trailing on the floor.

Color: The walls, the shelves and even the stairs themselves have all been painted in the same soft off-white to add further to the uniform look – the shelves almost disappear into the creamy background.

Floor: Instead of carpet, the floor is treated with a wash of diluted emulsion to give a limed effect and sealed with hard-wearing floor varnish.

TIP
Put up 'floating' shelves with concealed fittings for a streamlined effect.

Curtain raiser

Wardrobes aren't always the answer to clothes storage, especially if you're struggling with a small bedroom.

Hanging: Older houses often have chimneys in the bedrooms, which are great if you want character, not so good if what you want is the maximum space. Make a virtue out of the features you have by turning the alcoves either side into storage space. These spaces are not usually deep enough for tradi- tional built-in wardrobes, which would simply protrude into the room and eat up even more space. Instead take a trip to the nearest hardware store and stock up on the internal fittings for wardrobes and put up a rail at head height for all your hangers.

Shelves: The gaps above and below your hanging rail are prime shelf space. Hang up your longest clothes and mark the level they come to. Fit full-depth shelves below this level leaving enough room below the bottom shelf for shoes to sit on the floor.

Yet more shelves above the rail can be stacked with those things (like wedding hats and beach bags) that you need on an occasional basis.

Curtain: The least space-hungry way to enclose your wardrobe area is with a full-length curtain. Fix a curtain track to the ceiling and hang the curtain from it to keep everything dust-free.

Bits and pieces: A stack of shoeboxes covered in pretty toning wallpapers will fit neatly on the shelves and swallow up all manner of odds and ends such as undies, jewelery, handbags and scarves.

Box office

If your computer has to live in the living room make sure it can be hidden away at a moment's notice.

Wardrobe: Custom-made computer workstations are easily available but most come with a hefty price tag. Instead you could go the do-it-yourself route and convert a cheap and cheerful wardrobe into a stylish hideaway. Paint or wallpaper the outside to tone with the scheme of your room.

Shelves: Think about what you need to store in your cabinet and then plan the shelving to suit. A high shelf at the top of the cabinet is placed to allow just enough room for a few books, CD-roms and office extras like a hole punch and stapler. A full-depth shelf at waist height will take the computer monitor while the hard drive can sit in the bottom of the cabinet. Use drawer runners to fix an extra shelf below the monitor to take the keyboard.

Color: In a plain, pale room you can afford a flash of brilliant color when you open your workstation. Hot pink is a stimulating shade and bound to raise a smile when you fling back the door. Lightly sand then prime the surfaces and paint with gloss or eggshell for a hardwearing finish.

Filing: Pop a freestanding filing rack inside the bottom of the cabinet to keep everything close to hand. Plywood magazine files screwed to the inside of the door will hold stocks of paper, envelopes and your correspondence. Make sure they don't snag on any of the shelves when you close the cabinet.

TIP

Glue cork tiles inside one of the doors and paint to match the interior providing somewhere to pin notes, cards and inspiring images.

Step up to style

If you want one shining example of how to use the space under your stairs to brilliant effect, this has to be it.

Boxes: Serious storage starts with some serious planning. This space was drawn up on graph paper and a grid of boxes planned to fill the space entirely. The cabinet has then been built-in permanently so there are no dust-trap areas behind or below the shelving. The entire cabinet has been made to accommodate a huge collection of magazines and books.

Cabinet: This system is in an open-plan home where tidiness is essential as one messy area will make the whole flat seem cluttered. To the left, where the slope of the staircase ends, a large maple veneer cabinet has been added and holds shelves full of folded clothes and rack upon rack of shoes. Great care has gone into the construction of the cabinets so they are as beautiful as they are functional and the doors have been

veneered inside and out with maple. This kind of storage actively encourages you to be tidy as so much thought has gone into the design that it is no effort to use.

Color: The safest of the color cards has been played here and the whole apartment is painted in light-enhancing white. Adding pale wood tones and a completely plain and natural carpet makes the space seem to stretch out in front of you. The addition of one chair in navy blue breaks up this neutral scene.

Anywhere goes

Take whatever opportunities your home offers to build in some extra storage to make your life simpler and more organized.

Shoes: If you've ever totaled up the value of your clothes for insurance purposes you'll know how quickly the value of your shoes adds up. A pair of sneakers here, some strappy sandals there and, before you know it, there's hundreds (if not thousands) of dollars' worth kicking around in the bottom of your wardrobe. Having splashed the cash on the footwear it makes sense to create space to store them properly and keep them looking their best. Open your eyes to the potential of any space in your home, after all, shoes don't have to be in the bedroom. In this home a generous alcove in the bathroom has been pressed into service with floor-to-ceiling pigeon-holes, so you can see at a glance which pair you want to wear.

Bathroom cabinet: Storage has to be easy to use if you are going to stick with it and lead a tidy life. The bathroom cabinet around this sink has been designed with open shelves that take baskets of different sizes to hold toiletries and towels. Each basket can be lifted out and used on the counter-top in complete comfort or transported to the bedroom if necessary. Deep drawers are used to stash yet more bits and pieces and can be reached without bending.

Sink: The bowl-style glass sink takes up the minimum of space on the counter-top but allows plenty of room for washing. Taps coming out of the wall help to keep the surface clear.

Towel rail: A bamboo ladder used as a towel rail provides masses of space for towels to hang and air in this busy family bathroom.

Take aways

If you're in rented accommodation or planning to move soon you need simple storage without massive financial outlay.

Freestanding: Major fitted storage is only really worth the investment if you are going to be staying in a house for some years to get the benefits. Although plenty of storage will help sell a house it's unlikely to recoup the amount it cost when you sell up and move on. Better by far is to invest a smaller sum in freestanding pieces that you can pack up and take with you when you move.

Furniture: A chest of drawers is an essential in any room and small shelves above add height and visual punch as well as being somewhere to display favorite things. A low set of shelves slots into an unused corner and makes a home for clothes and a few shoes. Rather than leave it as plain open shelving which can give a cluttered and messy effect, a sheer white muslin cover has been added. With the front panel unrolled it makes a sleek and unobtrusive shape in the corner of the room.

Boxes: Every surface has been tidied of its clutter with the addition of a few pretty boxes that earn a place on show.

Color: An all-white color scheme is used here to great effect. The snowy scene is enlivened by small flashes of icy blue, including a shiny satin quilt covering half the bed.

Bay watch

If someone suggested using a window for storage, you'd think they were mad, right? Wrong!

Bay: There's something about the thought of a bay window that sends normally confident home decorators into a bit of a tizzy. They've got an undeserved reputation for being difficult to dress but can in fact be the best asset a room can have.

Shelving: Boxing in the area under a bay window can provide lots of space (think caravans and how much stuff gets stowed away under the seats) as long as you build in lift-up lids. Not only that but this storage doubles as a useful place to sit and read or use the telephone. Boxing in the bay entirely though, can break up the floor area and have the effect of making the room seem shorter. A cleverer option is to build a shaped seating and shelving area like the one shown here. It maintains the room's open and airy feel but still provides seating and a lot of shelf space for books and games. Even better, the cabinet is freestanding and can be pulled out if you need to get right up to the window to clean or paint it in comfort.

Curtains: Normally floor-length curtains are the most elegant, helping to make your windows look taller. With a window seat however, the curtains need to be cut shorter to glide neatly over the seat when they are closed. A fabric with slim vertical stripes helps to compensate for this lack of length.

TIP
Blinds fitted into the window recess would be even neater and allow the seat to be used in comfort when drawn.

Better by design

There are many ways to maximize the potential space in your existing home. As so often happens, the simplest ideas are best but sometimes these gems do not generate the space you need, so it could be time to call in the professionals.

Carpenters: For smaller jobs start by consulting a carpenter if you are in any doubt about your skills to tackle the job you have in mind. Personal recommendation remains the best way to find someone reputable – and good carpenters are out there, despite all the scary stories.

Interior designers: Professional interior designers are trained to analyze the way the internal space in your home is used and then improve it. If you can't see the solutions yourself, consider employing a designer to help you re-plan your space – it will be money well spent. Although many professionals only work on large commissions, others are prepared to take on smaller jobs. To find a qualified, professional designer contact the American Society of Interior Designers (ASID).

Architects: Do you dream of having a wonderfully designed home? Employing an architect is not a privilege of the extremely wealthy and if you are considering extensive remodeling of the interior of your home it makes sense to consult one early on. Trained to take a brief, they will also see the bigger picture to reveal ideas and solutions you may not have imagined were possible. They will also guide you through building contracts, planning permission or completely coordinate the project if you wish. The American Institute of Architects (AIA) can help you find an architect in your area.

TIP

Has your family changed since you moved into your house? When kids arrive or leave home your space needs change accordingly and you may not be making the most of what you have.

Open house

Knocking two rooms into one can be wonderfully space enhancing and give you a great sense of freedom in your home.

Lateral thinking: Before considering a costly addition, ask yourself the following questions: are you using the space you have in the best way? Is there an area in your home that you rarely use and could it be better used for another function? Will re-planning a room allow you space for something you don't already have – a play area perhaps?

Walls: Opening out two rooms into one or removing a partition wall into a hallway will give you an affordable taste of open-plan living. Do consult a carpenter or structural engineer before attempting to remove a wall yourself as it could be load-bearing. Linking a dining room and kitchen, a kitchen and sun room or a sitting room and hallway are all logical steps that will enhance the space available to you.

Colors: Consider the way that you decorate the new space. Keeping flooring and colors consistent throughout will link the areas and make them seem like one. Laying wooden flooring lengthways, running from one room into the other will also help unify the spaces.

Furniture: Building a bank of seating into a family kitchen is an efficient way of getting a dining area into the space. Lift-up seats conceal large spaces for big pans that would otherwise fill the wall cabinets. The dining table has wheels added so that it slides easily out of the way when the children need room for games.

TIP
You won't need planning permission to take down a wall but the alteration may need building regulations approval – consult your local planning office.

Full focus

Trying to claw back each and every inch of space in your home means re-evaluating each nook, cranny and feature. Every room needs a focal point but in a small home a traditional fireplace can be replaced with something far more space-friendly without sacrificing style.

Fireplace: If you have full central heating chances are that your fireplaces are simply attractive features rather than put to practical use. Removing the fireplace completely will free maximum wall space but leave the room without a focal point. A neat alternative is to convert the chimney breast to a display area that retains the overall feel of a fireplace. Instead of having a fire basket simply plaster the inside of the opening to make a niche that can be used for displays

or, in a dining room, have a wine rack fitted.

Mantelshelf: A floating ledge provides plenty of space for arranging an attractive collection of items. When the old fireplace has been removed, and before re-plastering the wall, fix a chunky wooden shelf at a suitable height using large mirror plates or straight metal brackets screwed to the back of the shelf and the wall. Plaster over the fixings to conceal and create the 'floating' effect.

Hearth: A fireplace that is purely for decoration has no need of a hearth and removing it will give you a little more valuable floor space. A very modern look is to plaster the wall flush down to the floor but you might prefer to bring the skirting board around the front of the chimney breast.

TIP
Solid fuel fireplaces that are in use must have a hearth for health and safety reasons. Some 'hole in the wall' type fires are approved for use without a hearth but check with the retailer when you buy.

Open wide

A redundant fireplace is a bit of a gift if you're looking to make the most of the space in your home.

Chimney breast: There are several creative ways to make more use of an unused fireplace. Some you'll be able to tackle yourself, others you'll need a handyman to do for you. Removing the fire surround and fire basket itself will give you a usable alcove that can be filled with shelves or fitted with doors to make an extra cabinet.

Open up: If you remove some of the wall above the original opening (it will need a lintel to support the remainder of the wall) it will create a really useful space that's great for stowing large appliances, like this fridge freezer, in a small kitchen diner.

Out with it: Removing a chimney breast altogether is definitely a job for professionals. You can't just take it out of a ground floor without substantial work to support the upstairs chimney breast and fireplace. A better idea in a small home might be to have the whole chimney removed right from ground level, up through the first floor and roof. This will give you at least a square yard of extra space in each room, free up an entire wall that you can then place furniture against and make the spaces easier to design.

TIP

If you open up a fireplace in a kitchen and use it to house your oven the ventilation fan above can vent straight into the original chimney saving you the expense and hassle of fitting ducting.

Hall's fair

A narrow hallway can give a cramped first impression of your home so it's time to do something about it.

Space: A hallway is a lovely feature if you have a big home with enough space in the hall to greet and say goodbye to guests. If it's little more than a mean corridor with half a dozen doors opening off it it's serving little practical purpose and adding nothing to the style of your home.

Doors: The first thing to consider is whether you need a door on every room that opens off the hall. Removing them will give a much better sense of space in your home and make planning room designs easier as you won't have to allow space for doors to open into.

Walls: More radical, but more effective would be to remove some walls, or at least have the door openings made wider, so the hall space is incorporated into your living area. This is a job for a structural engineer to assess and for a professional carpenter to carry out.

Decoration: Open-plan living calls for some coordinated thinking when it comes to decoration. What's called for is a palette of colors that you can happily live with throughout this opened-out space. Keep wall colors uniform or stick to subtly different tones of one color and take flooring right through. In areas such as a kitchen, where a carpet would not be appropriate, switch to a hard floor but in a similar tone to the flooring elsewhere for a seamless look.

Orderly office

A tiny room is all most people can spare as a dedicated office and takes a little special planning to make it work efficiently.

Desk: To create a desk with a usable sized surface, buy or make one to fit into a corner. These work well as you have work surface on either side of you and it's all within easy reach without leaning or stretching uncomfortably. This one has been constructed from thick MDF (medium density fiberglass), which is easy to work with as it has no grain. In a particularly narrow room take the desk right across from wall to wall to avoid leaving awkward little spaces at the end that are no use.

Filing: Small filing cabinets, which will slip under the ends of your desk will provide plenty of space for paperwork. Several small cabinets that can be tucked away are better than one or two taller ones in a room of such modest proportions. If there is room, one could always be left out alongside the desk to provide a little extra work surface for filing trays or reference books.

Computer: Push the computer monitor right back into the corner so it uses up the unreachable part of the desk. Your desk will need to be deep enough in the corner for the keyboard to sit comfortably in front of the monitor with space for your wrists to rest on the desk to avoid strain injuries.

Window: A study or office needs a window treatment to provide shade and stop glare on the monitor screen. A Venetian blind is neat and completely adjustable depending on the light level.

A warning!

A sun room tops the polls of the home improvement most people would like to make – and not without reason. Make this addition to your home and you'll enjoy space and light all year round.

Planning permission: Building aaaaaa sun room may require planning permission. You'll need to apply if your sun room will cover more than 50% of the garden, if you build within 6 ½' of the boundary and the highest point is 13' or more, or if the sun room will be closer to a public highway than your original house.

Building regulations: Sun rooms are generally exempt if they have a transparent or translucent roof, walls of at least 75% glazing, a floor area of no more than $98'^2$, are built at ground level and are separated from the main house by a wall or physical barrier. Various restrictions apply in different areas – check with your local authorities before going too far with your plans.

TIP
Mark out the space your sun room will occupy in your garden with canes to get an idea of the space it will use up and how much garden you will be left with.

Hot stuff

It's time to rethink your heating as standard radiators take up valuable space that you could put to better use.

Modern style: Replace old radiators with compact new ones, designed to either run along the floor at skirting-board height, spiral upwards into a corner or run vertically up the wall rather than along it.

Hot foot: Replace radiators with underfloor heating. Wall-mounted radiators get in the way of your furniture and removing them gives you more freedom when it comes to room design. Different systems are available working on either a thin electric element or a hot water pipe running under your tiles or other flooring. Electric heating costs around $40 per square yard, water-filled systems are around $75 per square yard.

Towel rails: In a bathroom or kitchen a towel rail radiator doubles as heating and storage space and provides a designer focus for a dull room. As well as straightforward electric radiators and those that connect to your central heating, there is a dual fuel option: cleverly designed to connect both to mains electricity and central heating so you have the choice of using the rail as a full radiator in winter or as a towel warmer.

Boiler: While you are thinking about your heating system it's time to look at your boiler. If it's old you'll be surprised at how small modern boilers are and if you have it changed you might be able to find a better, less obtrusive place for it to be sited.

The only way is up

Aim high if you've lofty ceilings and a desire for an extra room.

Platform: This is the way to go if you're lucky enough to have a home with high ceilings. To be really useful you should aim to include a proper staircase for easy access and building something like this is probably a job for a professional.

Stairs: An open-tread design has been chosen for this staircase to keep the effect airy. The lost corner under the stairs has cleverly been pressed into service as a little extra space to fill with shelves to stash books and the stereo.

Space: A seating area is ideal under a platform as the effect will be cosy and snug and if you are seated for most of the time you won't notice the lowering of the ceiling quite so much. A mezzanine like this is ideally suited to a spare bedroom, a study or even a children's playroom. Be sure to brief your carpenter if you are going to use it as a home gym as the equipment involved can be extremely heavy.

Color: In this room the wall has been painted an amazing midnight blue to play on the cosy feel while the mezzanine framework has been kept glossy and white to avoid it bearing down overhead. A squashy sofa was chosen for its low-rise proportions and natural calico covers help brighten the area.

TIP
Make sure you fit some sort of lighting under the mezzanine to give it a welcoming glow in the evening. Even this picture light will help.

Coming through

How does swapping an airing cabinet for 25% more bathroom space sound? Good? Then read on.

Boiler: A combi-boiler which heats water as you use it is a serious point to consider if you have a big family taking lots of showers and baths. Not only does it mean you never run out of water but it does away with the need for that bulky hot water tank that's lurking in the airing cabinet. And of course, if there's no need for the tank you can think again about what you do with the space it occupies. Of course, a cabinet this size provides lots of storage and that might be just what you need. On the other hand if it adjoins the kitchen or bathroom you might want to knock through and absorb the extra space into one of the hardest-working rooms in the house.

Storage: In this bathroom the wall has been taken down to bring the adjoining cabinet space into the bathroom. Small piers on either side support the RSJ that's been installed and make an interesting niche that's been fitted out with wall-to-wall storage. Simple laminate cabinets are used at ground level but a marble countertop ups the style stakes and adds plenty of glamour.

Mirror: Lining the alcove with mirror gives the impression of looking through into an adjacent room, an effect that's emphasized by the narrow opening. The mirror is actually fronting doors on push catches that conceal masses of extra cabinet space that's well out of reach of children.

Step to the side

Go back: No room at the side? Pushing the back of the house out into a sun room will give you the extra space you crave. This kind of sun room addition is wonderful as a kitchen and dining space, as the natural light levels are excellent.

Color: In a room with such great light you can afford to be a bit bolder with color without any risk of the stronger shades making the space seem poky. However, choose the paler, receding shades and you'll simply emphasize the impression of space.

Time: So completely pushed for time that you can't begin to think about organizing a major renovation? Call in a project manager – a new breed of professionals who will help busy owners with home improvements, giving advice on planning, building regulations and design economics. Check your telephone directory and local papers for a project manager local to you.

TIP
Need finance for your project? Check out what you can afford to borrow before briefing anyone on your needs.

Loft living

Buoyant house prices mean you may find it makes more financial sense to extend your existing home rather than move.

Budget: If you think that extending is out of reach, do some math homework first. Add the cost of moving from your existing property – conveyancing, survey, search fees, real estate agents' fees, removals – to the cost of buying a larger property. An average loft conversion costs around $35,000 and basement conversions from $100,000, so it may make sense to stay put.

Loft space: You've done your homework and concluded that 'up' it is! Start by getting an architect to draw up the plans for your loft. When it comes to employing a carpenter or specialist loft company, get at least three quotes and look at examples of their work or talk to recent customers, before you make your final choice.

Bedroom: An extra bedroom is one of the most straightforward loft conversions and safest in terms of investment – estate agents reckon that a fourth bedroom is a valuable feature in a family home. As a rule you do not need planning permission for a loft conversion unless you want to put a window in the roof that faces the road.

Storage: The space under the eaves has valuable storage potential and let's face it, the roof height means it can be used for little else. Custom-built storage here makes sense and is worth designing and budgeting for at the initial planning stages.

Dining out

If you like to entertain, a sun room is the perfect place. Imagine a warm summer's evening with guests spilling out onto the lawn or a winter dinner with candles twinkling in lanterns outside in the garden – magical!

Ventilation: In summer, over-heating is the one problem you have to tackle in a sun room and prevention starts with the design of the structure itself. High-level vents, either manual or automatic, will let the hot air rise and flow out of the roof. Low-level windows that can be opened will help the flow of air through, drawing cooler air in at the bottom of the room.

Blinds: In a sun room that's used as a dining or living room, blinds are more about shade and insulation than they are about privacy. Pleated blinds can be made to fit the contours of your roof exactly and will go a long way to regulating the temperature which can rise quickly even on a cool spring day if the sun is out for long periods. Fabrics are available which will keep you cool in summer but also insulate the room in winter helping to make it usable all year round. Fit blinds on the side windows and you've got even more control over the temperature and they will also help shade expensive furniture from the fading effect of the sun.

Color: Neutral or natural flooring works well in a sun room making a smooth transition from indoors to outdoors. Your blinds become your wall color so choose them to harmonize with the green scene beyond. Here, a fruity design complements the colors of the furnishings and the green of the plants outside.

TIP
Arrange furniture so there is a clear walkway from the house to the garden so you don't have to pick your way around things.

Night life

If you're going to the bother of adding a sun room make sure you get the maximum use out of it all year round.

Heating: One common mistake is to build a sun room on the tightest of budgets and not bother adding the things, such as heating and ventilation, which will make it useful all year round. During summer a lack of heat isn't an issue and, in fact, in most sun rooms you will only need supplementary heat for a few months in the middle of winter. Rather than rely on freestanding gas heaters (smelly) or electric fan heaters (noisy and expensive to run), have an extra radiator fitted that works off the main central heating system.

Air-conditioning: At the other end of the scale you might want to consider air-conditioning if the room is to be a key space in your home rather than a room that's used sporadically.

Furniture: Invest in a good sofa bed and your new sun room could quick-change into a dreamy guest room that no one will want to leave. Comfort is a priority both in sofa mode and made up as a bed so make sure you try it out before you buy. Don't be shy, ask to pull it out as a bed, slip your shoes off and lie down. Make yourself comfortable and stay there for at least five minutes to make sure it really is comfortable – after all you're expecting your guests to lie there for eight hours a night!

Blinds: Privacy is paramount if people are to sleep in a sun room and pleated roof blinds are a great starting point. Team them with vertical blinds which can be fully closed, opened by degree to filter light in or drawn right back when you want to take in the view of your garden.

Going underground

If you really don't want to move but are desperate for more space dig deep and convert your basement.

Value: If you have a high-value property and you have already extended every other way you can, it can be cost-effective to convert your basement. When you add up the costs of moving it can come to a frightening amount. Yet you could convert an existing basement into a whole extra floor of high-quality living accommodation for around $120,000. Get a qualified architect or specialist basement conversion firm to assess the feasibility and cost and check with your local realtor whether the cost can be recovered on resale.

What's involved: Generally a basement conversion will involve excavating earth to make enough headroom and underpinning the existing foundations. You also need to waterproof the walls, lay a concrete slab floor and re-route the drainage. Costs for this type of conversion are between $210 and $270 per square foot – or $100,000 to $135,000 – as it is very labor-intensive. The work will take at least four months, but you should be able to live in your house without too much disruption. You will need permission for external alterations, such as putting in a lightwell, so don't go ahead with the project until you have received approval. Employ an architect through ASA's client advisory service or go for a specialist basement contractor and the regulations will be taken care of while you concentrate on the interior.

Neighbors: You will need to employ a party-wall surveyor to agree the work with the neighbors, and you should allow $1500 to cover this.

TIP
You may not want the full expense of a basement conversion, but would a cellar help? Creating a cellar is a smaller (but still significant) job and it could provide storage for the whole family.

On reflection

Mirrors don't have to line whole walls to be an effective space-enhancing tool.

Mix and match: Fill an entire wall with an eclectic collection of mirrors – the effect will be similar to using one large mirror, and is more unusual. Scour junk shops and yard sales for your collection. You'll be surprised that even the cheapest finds look good used as a group. Vary the size and intersperse modern, traditional, plain and ornate styles for maximum decorative effect.

Border: Create an unusual border by using alternative small rectangles of mirror with painted strips of plywood. Ask a glazier to cut ⅛"-thick mirror off-cuts about 6" wide. Cut strips of ⅛"-thick plywood the same size. Sand the rough edges of the plywood smooth, then prime and paint the strips. Draw a chalk line on the wall as a guide for the base of your border, then use tile adhesive to glue on the mirrors and ply.

TIP
If you'd prefer a theme for your mirrors you could paint all the frames to match in a color to contrast with your walls.

Hidden depths

Once you start looking it's surprising how much spare space you can find in a tiny kitchen and it's all there just waiting for you to use!

Plinths: Many kitchen manufacturers are waking up to the idea that we don't all have the kitchen of our dreams. Clever developments include drawers that fit into the plinth level below the base cabinets. Also look out for slim heaters (sometimes called kickspace heaters) that fit into the same space and are perfectly adequate to heat a kitchen and which will allow you to gain some valuable wall space by getting rid of a bulky radiator.

Drawers: Sacrificing one drawer in your kitchen will give you the space to have an extra pull-out worktop or even a built-in ironing board which extends ready for use in a matter of seconds.

Chill out

Need somewhere to escape and chill out? Put a simple shed in a quiet corner of the garden and turn it into a tranquil summer house.

Style: A Japanese-inspired shed is the perfect space for a little afternoon meditation. Disguise an ugly felt roof with bamboo screening which is available on long rolls from garden centers and make a trellis of thick bamboo canes up the side and another of thinner canes across the window. Let sweetly-scented jasmine trail its way around the window and grow a hardy bamboo alongside.

Deck: Make yourself a little patio area where you can sit outside and catch some sun. Simply place wooden decking tiles straight on the ground.

TIP
In winter when it's too cold to use your summer house pile it up with all the garden furniture that needs to be stored somewhere dry.

Inside: A bench, an incense burner, some cushions and a book are all you need to complete your private haven. Choose silky fabrics printed with flowers, leaves and birds.

Room for one more

Turn a single into a double and make more guests welcome.

Bed: In a single guest room it seems a shame not to use the space under the bed to the fullest . No one minds a slightly tight squeeze in the bedroom if they're only staying for a night or two but they will mind cramming into a bed that's too small or having to sleep on the sofa. Check out the latest bed designs that are available and you'll be able to offer everyone a comfortable stay. A single bed with another that slides out on castors is ideal – especially in a teenager's room where sleepovers are a must. Some stay at low level, others pop up on legs so the two parts can be pushed together to make a generous double.

Bedding: Extra beds mean extra linen and duvets. A blanket chest with an upholstered lid is a great way to make extra storage and will double as a dressing-table seat or even a bedside table.

TIP
Piled with cushions and bolsters a simple divan makes a comfortable sofa during the day.

Shelf life

Bedside tables, with their tiny drawers, provide precious little storage space but there is a clever alternative.

Shelf: Do away with your mean little bedside table and put up a floating shelf each side of the bed to take an alarm clock, books and a trinket or two. You might be able to find kits for this type of shelf, if not, they're simple to make using a thick wooden shelf. Drill deep holes in the back of the shelf and corresponding holes in the wall. Cut a metal rod to length and glue into both the shelf and the wall to support the shelf.

Trunk: The space you've freed where the bedside table would have stood can now be home to a large trunk which can store all your out-of-season clothes or bedding. A charming alternative to the trunk would be a stack of vintage suitcases which would give even more storage opportunities.

TIP
Rather than overloading your shelf double up with another above it.

Snuggle up

If the TV's always on in the sitting room you need a space to call your own when you want to sit and read.

Find room: Having your own quiet corner where you can retreat with a magazine or book might seem like an unachievable luxury but you don't need much space, just a little imagination. The area under the stairs is ideal but put your mark on it before someone else earmarks it as an office or wardrobe!

Relax: Choose a small armchair that will look in proportion in this compact space. No high backs or fancy scrolled arms here please, just a simple shape in a pale fabric and pale wood legs that keep the mood fresh and airy.

Storage: Add a couple of shelves tucked high up under the slope of the stairs so it leaves you plenty of headroom. When there are small children around, the higher the better so small hands can't get hold of your favorite read.

TIP
You might want to add a standard lamp or clip-on shelf light to brighten the area for reading.

Mind the gap

The space under a staircase is ripe for exploitation. Think about what storage or furniture you can build in there to help your home.

Kitchen: In this home the stairs go up alongside the kitchen and although the headroom in this corner is limited no chances have been missed to build in a little extra storage. The base cabinets are taken right along under the slope of the stairs and the awkward space above is pressed into service for a modular wine rack. This is also the perfect excuse for keeping supplies well stocked. An empty wine rack doesn't look half as good!

Boxes: Even if you don't go as far as building in furniture the space under your stairs can still be made to swallow up a load of clutter. The advantage of using boxes to store things under the stairs is that you can scale them down to utilize every inch of space. Archive boxes from large stationers are a good place to start as they're big and have handles making them manoeuvrable. Either paint them or cover them with coordinating wrapping or wallpaper to make an eye-catching display.

TIP
This is a great place for bulky bed linens, table linens and towels which eat up cabinet space.

Under cover

It's one thing stuffing things under your bed to get them out of sight, but it's quite another to turn it into a well-designed storage space.

Shoes: A shoe-strewn house is part and parcel of family life, but that doesn't mean you have to like it. The solution is a tray on four castors that you simply hook out from under the bed with your foot. This one is made from a piece of ½"-thick MDF (medium density fiberglass) with a wooden batten glued and screwed around the edge to make a lip. With a coat of white paint and a wheel screwed to each corner it's ready for action.

Clothes: A similar arrangement, but with the addition of deeper sides, is ideal for jumpers and other bulky items that don't easily fit into drawers. If you have cats make sure the boxes only just fit under the bed so the cats can't crawl in over the top and make a nest!

On the shelf

Take a cheap and cheerful bookshelf cabinet and turn it into an eye-catching storage system for kitchenware.

Hanging space: Under the top shelf of the cabinet a large cup hook has been screwed into each upright. A length of dowel, cut to fit to make a hanging rail for utensils and pans, can simply be hung from the hooks. Below the second shelf a double row of smaller cup hooks has been added to take mugs, jugs and tea towels.

Racks: Check out the kitchen fittings section of your local hardware store and you'll find all sorts of little racks that are designed to slot onto cabinet shelves to give you extra compartments for items like spices. One of these slotted onto the center shelf of this cabinet holds a box of eggs (which should be stored at room temperature).

Hideaway: The sort of springy wire that net curtains are hung from has been stretched across the front of the bottom shelf. With the addition of a neat PVC curtain (eyelets save sewing a channel for the heading), a storage space is created for the things that you don't want to keep on show.

Color: Priming the cabinet and painting it clinical glossy-white serves two purposes: firstly it creates an easily cleaned surface that can be wiped down, secondly the glossy finish of the paint creates another light-catching surface in the room and brightens the space.

Lose and gain

If you're prepared to lose a few inches off the back of a worktop you could gain high-rise storage.

Shelving: By adding a ready-made pigeon-hole storage cabinet (originally intended as a CD rack) to this run of worktops it has created four times as much space. Everything that a couple needs for everyday, including jugs, mugs, glasses, bowls, coffee maker, salt and pepper shakers and teapot are all here just an arm's reach away. Rather than fit a carousel into the corner cabinet of the kitchen the space has been left open to provide shelving and display space in one. The wall shelves have been given a chunky new look to match the shelf in the corner cabinet by tacking 1"-wide MDF (medium density fiberglass) strips along the front. Repetition is the key to open plan shelving. The coffee makers and mugs give a pleasing rhythm to this display.

Color: All the shelves, old and new, have been painted in sparkling white to tie them into the scheme.

Lighten up

Is your carpet cramping your style? If it's too dark it could be.

Before: Take a look at the room below. It's got most things right, the walls are pale, the striped curtains give an impression of height without dominating, the sofa is nicely neutral and piled with cushions in an interesting mix of textures and shades. So what's wrong?

After: Nothing has changed here apart from the deep blue carpet, but just look how much bigger the room appears to be. With the carpet ripped up and pale laminate flooring in its place all the other space-enhancing tricks suddenly have a chance to shine. If you can't replace a dark claustrophobic carpet you can hide as much of it as possible under a light and lovely rug.

TIP
Bare wood underfoot too chilly for you? Add a soft chenille rug but just make sure it's the same pale tone as the floor.

Now you see it

Get to grips with the effect color can have if you want to 'space out' your home.

Contrast: Sharp contrasts in color are excellent if you want to draw attention to something. If you'd rather everything blended in for a seamless, spacious feel you have to reduce contrast and go for subtle shades of one color to create your scheme. In this tiny sitting room the sofa is well placed in the crook of the stairs to make the most of the available space. By replacing the original deep blue upholstery with new tailored yellow covers to match the wall, it appears to melt into its surroundings.

Pattern: Bold designs are also to be avoided in tight spaces. Instead go for subtle woven designs such as damasks or printed patterns in shades of one color to add a little visual interest.

TIP
If you're going to the bother and expense of loose covers make sure you choose a machine-washable fabric – especially if there are kids and pets in the house.

Window wise

If you need to dress your windows keep it simple and follow these tips for maximum space-enhancing effect.

Pare down: Throw out that chintz (and any other over-the-top drapery) if the room is not overlooked – especially if the view outside is good. This will maximize light in the room, show off a lovely window and lead your eye straight outside, increasing the sense of spaciousness within.

Be neat: Roman blinds, shutters or sheer blinds are all top options for rooms that need a little privacy. Repeat the color used on adjacent walls for the window treatment and if using fabric, create interest with texture or an unusual trim along the bottom instead. Hang your blinds as high as possible on your window frame so that they clear the glass when raised.

TIP
If you like the luxury of curtains keep them simple! Mount them on a streamlined pole or track or even a fashionable tension wire and eyelet system and make sure there's enough room to pull them right back off the window during the day.

Cabinet love

Got a broom cabinet? Then you could have a utility room if you play your space cards right.

Plumbing: To create a mini-utility room you'll need a cold water supply to the cabinet, a power socket and access to a drain. With that sorted you're ready to go.

Appliances: Most washing machines and dryers can be stacked one on top of the other to cram more into a small space. A special stacking kit, available from most electrical retailers, will let you stack things safely – even when the washing machine is on its wildest spin! If you don't have a condensing tumble-dryer you will need to add a duct to vent the damp air to the outside, just as you would in a kitchen.

Shelving: Fixing a slatted shelf above the appliances means there's room for cleaning materials to be stashed away. Hooks on the inside of the door accommodate dustpan and brushes. Taller things like the ironing board and mops will tuck away down one side.

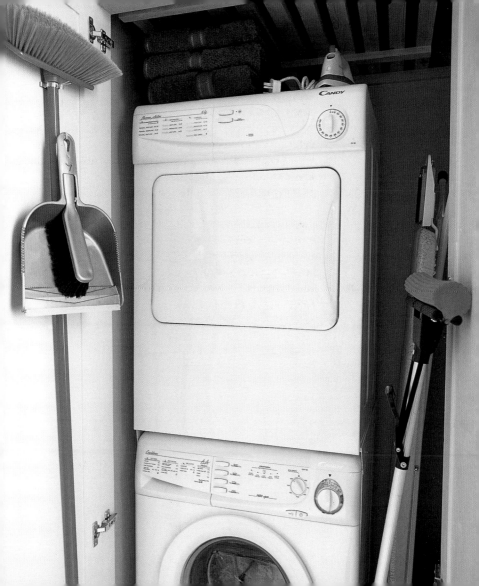

Smart storage

Louvred doors aren't exactly the height of fashion but can be reinvented to make storage a breeze.

CDs: Left unchecked CDs tend to migrate all over the house (and car!). Make a home for them and do away with floor-hogging boxes and towers. This rack started life as a wooden louvre door that was cut down to size with the bottom rail refitted to finish it off neatly.

Paint: The old varnish was sanded down to key the surface and reveal the original wood around the edges then it was given a coat of emulsion. When dry, the emulsion was sanded back along the edges to show the wood and give a distressed finish. A coat of wax protects the finish and the whole rack can be hung on the wall with a couple of brass mirror plates.

Into the fold

Neat furniture will make life more comfortable when space is at a premium.

Fold it: A kitchen can be persuaded to accommodate a breakfast area if you shop cleverly for the right furniture. A gate-leg table that folds down and pushes against the wall allows free flow around the room during the day and offers an extra work surface. If the chairs fold, stack or hang on the wall when not in use so much the better. Even more economical with space is a table that's hinged to the wall and simply folds down flat when not needed.

Space: Other space-saving ideas for kitchens include cabinets with roller or sliding doors that need no extra room to open into, two-in-one appliances such as a washer/dryer which saves the space of one appliance under the worktop and stackable appliances such as fridges and freezers which make use of the height of the room.

TIP
Integrated appliances which fit behind doors to match your cabinets give a sleeker look than freestanding ones.

Straight up

If floor space is what you're short of think laterally – or rather, vertically.

Chest: Seek out pieces of furniture of the right proportions to fit the space you have. Just as in a city where high-rise offices help squeeze more into a small area, tall but slender cabinets and chests will pack storage space into your home. A chest like this with several graduated drawers that start small at the top and get progressively bigger at the bottom is very versatile for all sorts of belongings.

Mirror: There's always room for a little row of mirrors near or opposite a window to help boost the light levels. Above a high chest like this one they double as a make-up area saving the need for a separate dressing table.

Rack it up

If pots and pans fill acres of space in your kitchen cabinets get them out of the way on an overhead rack.

Materials: This modern take on a traditional drying rack is made from a piece of untreated garden trellis, a length of rope and a little leftover paint – simple!

Make it: Cut the trellis down to the size you want with a handsaw then sand it smooth all over. Paint with two coats of white emulsion and leave to dry. Fix four steel or brass screw hooks to a joist in the ceiling. Position the rack above a worktop or island cabinet where you won't obstruct the headroom. Cut the rope into four equal pieces, tie one to each corner of the rack and then to a hook in the ceiling. Chain would work just as well if you prefer.

Hang up: Use S-hooks with blunt ends to suspend pans, utensils and dried herbs from your rack.

More is more

The right accessories can double the amount you can get into a cabinet.

Rail: A built-in cabinet with a single hanging rail isn't a good use of space. Chances are that the things you hang leave lots of wasted space above and below which could be utilized with the addition of a few extra shelves and racks.

Go up: If there's space above your hanging rail fit one or two extra shelves so that things you only use occasionally can be tucked out of the way. This cabinet goes one better by dividing the space completely and adding an extra cabinet on top which is ideal for suitcases and other large lightweight items.

Hang it: These canvas hanging racks are widely available and if you haven't tried them yet you don't know what you're missing. Slipped onto a hanging rail they turn about 8" of your wardrobe into the equivalent of a chest of drawers.

TIP
Add one canvas rack for folded clothes and another to take shoes.

204

A bit on the side

If you sew, make models or enjoy games with the family you'll know that hobbies create lots of little bits and pieces that need compartmentalized storage for safe-keeping.

Console table: In this space that doubles as a sewing room and dining room every inch of space has been exploited. Rows and rows of filing boxes hold fabric samples, threads, buttons and trims and are stacked in regimented order under the table. By filling the space entirely the effect is more of a large chest of drawers and looks much more orderly and intentional than a single stack of boxes would. If you'd rather not see the boxes, a floor-length cloth, a fitted fabric cover or a row of roller blinds under the front edge of the table would all make stylish disguises.

Display: In the evening with the table set for dinner the filing boxes are barely noticeable. Instead the artful display of glass and ceramics in front of the huge mirror catches the eye and the attention.

Under cover

Disguise ugly radiators and build yourself a smart shelf at the same time.

The look: Radiators are seldom features to be admired unless you've spent hundreds of dollars on stylish Italian jobs. A neat cover will draw a veil over the look of your old radiators and make a display area while still allowing heat to circulate well.

Make it: Cut a top, two sides and a front from ¾" MDF (medium density fiberglass) and cut away a small piece at the back of each side so it will sit neatly over the skirting board. Cut a large oval hole in the front for ventilation and shape the bottom edge. Cut a piece of wire mesh to fit over the hole and use a staple gun or tacks to fit it to the back of the MDF. Drill, screw and glue the pieces together and fix to the wall with mirror plates.

Finish: Paint the cover with a couple of coats of eggshell or gloss paint in the same shade as the wall.

WHERE TO BUY:

ONE-STOP SHOPS

BED, BATH AND BEYOND
Furniture, linen, window
dressings and lighting.
Tel: 800 GO BEYOND
www.bedbathandbeyond.com

CRATE AND BARREL
Selection of contemporary
beds, as well as linens and
storage solutions.
www.crateandbarrel.com

HELTON
Furniture, linen, window
dressings and lighting.
Tel: 866 4 HELTEN
ww.helten.com

IKEA
Affordable flatpack furniture;
furnishings, fabrics and
lighting.
Tel: 516 681 4532
www.ikea-usa.com

LAURA ASHLEY
Classic and country-style bedding, fabrics, window dressings, lighting and paints.
Tel: 800 463 8075
www.laura-ashleyusa.com

LINENS'N THINGS
Affordable brand name
housewares for every room.
Tel: 866 568 7378
www.lnt.com

PIER ONE
Furniture, linen, window
dressings and lighting, with
an Asian flair.
Tel: 800 245 4595
www.pier1.com

FURNITURE

BAKER
Traditional, rattan, bamboo
and wood furniture.
800 662 4847
www.bakerfurniture.com

BUBBLE FURNITURE
Fun, colorful inflatable furniture. Great for extra company.
Tel: 800 704 9684
www.bubblefurniture.com

BOMBAY
Exotic furniture collections and accessories for the entire home.
800 829 7789
www.bombay.com

CLUB FURNITURE
Couches and chairs in leather or with slipcovers. Also a wide range of ottomans and sectionals.
Tel: 888 378 8383
www.clubfurniture.com

CRATE AND BARREL
Selection of contemporary beds, as well as linens and storage solutions.
Tel: 800 967 6696
www.crateandbarrel.com

DESIGN CONCEPTS UNLIMITED
Contemporary furniture of every room in the house.
www.dcuinc.com

EDDIE BAUER HOME
The classic Eddie Bauer casual style comes to the home in this collection of fine furniture.
Tel: 800 625 7935
www.eddiebauer.com

ETHAN ALLAN
Contemporary collection for all rooms.
Tel: 888 EAHELP1
www.ethanallan.com

GEORGE SMITH
Traditional sofas, chairs and chaises in a wide variety of collections.
Tel: 212 226 4747

HANCOCK AND MOORE
Leather chairs, sofas sectionals and sleepers in a choice of colors.
Tel: 800 300 2359
www.hancockandmoore.com

J.M. PAQUET
Bedroom and living room furniture, linens and slipcovers.
Tel: 323 549 9280
www.jmpaquet.com

LA-Z-BOY
This old stand-by has gotten a new look. They still carry a wide range of recliners, and now sofas and upright chairs as well.
www.lazboy.com

FURNITURE

FURNITURE

LEVITZ
Reasonably priced collections for the home, including a wide range of collections and designs for kids.
Tel: 888 538 2558 (east coast)
866 LEVITZ (west coast)
www.levitz.com

LL BEAN
A choice of collections, including futons and rattan furniture for the entire home.
Tel: 800 441 5713
www.llbean.com

LOST MOOSE
Rustic wood and iron furniture for the living room and bedroom.
888 253 6466

MODERN HOME
Modern bedroom and living room furniture, lighting and accessories.
Tel: 520 747 1729
www.modernhome.com

MUSEUM OF MODERN ART
Modern art prints and posters, glassware, furniture and more designed by some of the top modern artists.
Tel: 800 884 2212
www.moma.org

MONTANA LOG OUTFITTERS
Rustic log furniture for the bedroom and living room.
Tel: 877 590 69371
www.montanalogoutfitters.com

PLANUM FURNITURE
Contemporary furniture collections as well as entertainment and wall units.
www.planumfurniture.com

POTTERY BARN
High-quality furniture, wood and upholstered, fabric and leather for the entire home.
Tel: 888 779 5176
www.potterybarn.com

RESTORATION HARDWARE FURNITURE
From a home furnishing giant, a chain of contemporary furniture for the entire house.
Tel: 800 762 1005
www.restorationhardware.com

RETRO MODERN
Online shop for retro furnishings for the living room and bar, as well as retro lighting and accessories.
www.retromodern.com

ROOM AND BOARD
Furniture for adult and kids
bedrooms, as well as living
rooms and storage.
Tel: 800 486 6554
www.roomandboard.com

SEAMANS
Wide range of collections and
selections for all rooms in a
variety of styles and finishes.
Children's furniture also
available.
Tel: 800 445 2503
www.seamans.com

AMERICAN STANDARD
Sinks, faucets and accessories
in a wide range of modern
styles.
Tel: 800 442 1902
www.americanstandard-us.com

AQUAWORKS
Sinks and faucets, cabinets
and whirlpools.
Tel: 877 495 2111
www.aquaworks.com

BATES AND BATES
A wide collection of sinks in
metals, stone, ceramic and
stainless steel.
Tel: 800 726 7680
www.batesandbates.com

STICKLEY
Furniture for the entire house
in a variety of wood finishes
and upholstery.
Tel: 315 682 5500
www.stickley.com

TEMA
Furniture for all rooms,
including the home office.
Rugs and leather selections
also available..
Tel: 800 895 8362
www.tema-usa.com

BATH DEPOT
A wide collection of sinks,
faucets and toilets.
Tel: 800 769 BATH
www.bathdepot.com

BATHS.COM
Bathtubs and bathroom fixture
online. A variety of styles and
colors. Auction style.
www.baths.com

BIDET 2000
Toilets, bidets and travel
bidets. Also, sower toilets.
Tel: 877 852 2823
www.bidet-2000.com

FURNITURE

FIXTURES AND FAUCETS

FIXTURES AND FAUCETS

BLANCO
Stylish German-made sinks, taps and waste disposal units.
www.blanco-america.com

DELTA FAUCETS
Well known purveyors of sinks and faucets with a design-your-own-faucet option.
www.deltafaucet.com

HANSGROHE
A selection of massaging showerheads, faucets and wallbars.
Tel: 800 334 0455
www.hangrohe-usa.com

HOME DEPOT
Wide range of sinks, taps, cabinets and faucets for the DO-IT-YOURSELF set.
Tel: 800 430 3376
www.homedepot.com

KOHLER
Wide range or sinks and faucets in the most popular styles.
www.kohler.com

KWC FAUCETS
Faucets and sinks to fit any decor.
Tel: 877 592 3287
www.kwcfaucets.com

LOWES
Wide range of sinks, taps, cabinets and faucets. Also, water heaters, pipes and tanks for the DO-IT-YOUR-SELF set.
Tel: 800 44 LOWES
www.lowes.com

MOEN
Designer-style sinks in stainless steel and other popular material with many collections to choose from.
Tel: 800 BUY MOEN
www.moen.com

PRICE PFISTER
Ceramic and stainless steel faucets and sinks.
Tel: 800 PFAUCET
www.pricepfister.com

STONE FOREST
Handcrafted granite sinks.
Tel: 888 682 2987
www.stoneforest.com

VINTAGE TUB AND BATH
Vintage clawfoot tubs, showers, sinks and toilets.
Tel: 877 868 1369
www.vintagetub.com

WATERWORKS
Plumbing, fixtures, tubs
and sinks.
Tel: 800 998 BATH

BALL AND BALL
Hearth sets, grates, andirons
and fireplace cleaners.
Tel: 800 257 3711
www.ballandball.com

HEAT-N-GLO
Design your own artificial
fireplace. Indoor and outdoor.
Tel: 888 743 2887
www.heatnglo.com

LENNOX HEARTH PRODUCTS
Fireplaces, insets, stoves
and accessories.
www.lennoxhearthproducts.com

LOWES
Grates, glass fireplace doors,
gas logs, log racks, hearth
sets and more.
tel: 800 44 LOWES
www.lowes.com

WHITEHAUS
Wide collection of sinks in
metals and ceramics.
Tel: 800 527 6690
www.whitehaus.com

**MAJESTIC VERMONT
CASTINGS**
A variety of indoor and
outdoor fireplace solutions.
Tel: 905 670 7777
www.myownfireplace.com

REGENCY
contemporary styled wood-
burning and gas fueled fireplaces, fireplace inserts and
stoves.
www.regency-fire.com

TEMCO
Offers both woodburning
and gas fireplaces in a
variety of styles.
www.temcofireplaces.com

FIXTURES AND FAUCETS

FIREPLACES AND FITTINGS

PAINTS

ACE HARDWARE
Paint and paint supplies
including stencils and
painting advice.
Tel: 630 990 6600
www.acehardware.com

BENJAMIN MOORE
A wide selection of indoor and
outdoor paints and stains in
many colors and finishes.
Tel: 800 344 0400
www.benjaminmoore.com

BIOSHIELD
Solvent free and water based
house paint for a healthier
household. Many colors and
finishes available.
Tel: 800 621 2591
www.ecopaint.com

DUTCH BOY
Well-known for their interior
and exterior paint, this
company offers a wide
variety of colors and finishes.
Tel: 800 828 5669
www.dutchboy.com

FULLER O'BRIEN
Quality paint with affordable
prices in a wide selection of
colors and finishes.
www.fullerpaint.com

GLIDDEN
Well-known for their paint, this
company offers a wide variety
of colors and finishes.
Tel: 800 GLIDDEN
www.gliddenpaint.com

HOME DEPOT
Major retail outlet carrying
many designer paint brands
as well as lower priced ones.
Tel: 800 430 3376
www.homedepot.com

BLONDER HOME ACCENTS
Wallpaper for for every decor in many shades and fabrics.
Tel: 800 321 4070
www.blonderwall.com

BREWSTER WALLCOVERING COMPANY
They carry a wide selection of contemporary wallcoverings, borders and fabrics.
Tel: 800 366 1700
www.brewsterwallcovering.com

EISENHART WALLCOVERINGS
A wide range of wallcoverings and fabrics from playful for the kids to elegant for you.
Tel: 800 931 WALL
www.eisenhartwallcoverings.com

HOME DEPOT
A major retail outlet for all your home improvement needs, they carry many different brands and patterns in wallcoverings.
Tel: 800 430 3376
www.homedepot.com

F SCHUMACHER & CO.
A wide selection of wallpapers, rugs and fabrics for every decor and every room.
www.fschumacher.com

IMPERIAL HOME DECOR GROUP
Wallpaper and borders in many different styles for every room.
Tel: 888 608 5943
www.ihdg.com

INTERIOR MALL
This is an online source for all you interior decorating needs. Order online on via telephone.
Tel: 800 590 5884
www.interiormall.com

SEABROOK
A vast array of floral and country patterns to pretty up your home.
Tel: 800 238 9152
www.seabrookwallcoverings.com

SHERWIN WILLIAMS
Well-known for their paint, check out their collection of wallpaper and borders.
www.sherwinwilliams.com

VILLAGE HOME
Wallpaper and borders in many materials including fabrics and vinyls.
www.villagehome.com

WALLPAPER AND FABRICS

WINDOW TREATMENTS

BED BATH AND BEYOND
Window hardware, curtain panels, sheers, and bed canopies.
Tel: 800 GO BEYOND
www.bedbathandbeyond.com

HUNTER DOUGLAS
Vertical and horizontal blinds in many styles, colors and materials.
Tel: 800 937 7895
www.hunterdouglas.com

KESTREL
Interior and exterior wooden shutters and blinds. Also carry wooden hurricane shutters.
Tel: 800 494 4321
www.diyshutters.com

LEVOLOR
A wide range of window shades, mini-blinds, vertical blinds and other window treatments in a wide range of materials.
www.levolor.com

NORTHERN BLINDS
Wood and faux wood blinds, roller curtains, woven shadings.
Tel: 877 861 5023
www.northernblinds.com

RESTORATION HARDWARE
Lighting solutions for every room and every decor.
Tel: 800 762 1005
www.restorationhardware.com

RUE DE FRANCE
Window decor with a French country theme.
www.ruedefrance.com

SMITH AND NOBLE
Wood blinds, Durawood blinds, natural Roman shades and shutters and much more.
Tel: 800 560 0027
www.smithandnoble.com

ARMSTRONG

Linoleum and vinyl in a selection of wood and stone, smooth or textured.
Tel: 800 233 3823
www.armstrong.com

CARPET INNOVATIONS

Sisal, coirs, wool seagrass and jute flooring.
Tel: 800 457 4457
www.carpetinnovations.com

CLASSEN

A large selection of wood laminate flooring.
Tel: 800 834 8664
www.classenusa.com

E.Z. ORIENTAL INC.

Bamboo flooring in several finishes.
Tel: 888 395 8887
www.bamboofloor.net

HEMPHILLS RUGS AND CARPETS

Rugs, sisal and seagrass, shag rugs and rugs from around the world. Woven vinyl flooring.
Tel: 949 722 7224
www.rugsandcarpets.com

JELINEK GROUP

Finished and nonfinished cork floors in several colors, tree and environment friendly.
Tel: 716 439 4644
online ordering:
www.corkstore.com

WITEX FLOORING

Natural wood and wood laminate flooring in many styles.
Tel: 800 948 3987
www.witexusa.com

FLOOR COVERINGS

LIGHTING

ALTAMIRA LIGHTING
Unique metal and resin table and floor lamps with unique shades and finishes.
Tel: 401 245 7676
www.aliamiralighting.com

BLOOMING LIGHTS
Unique lighting with hand-made metal mesh lampshades in copper, brass, and stainless, featuring flower shapes. All items are made-to-order.
Tel: 800 295 0559
www.bloominglights.com

CRATE AND BARREL
Huge range of light fixtures, from traditional to cutting-edge.
Tel: 800 967 6696
www.crateandbarrel.com

DESIGN WITHIN REACH
Contemporary desk, floor, and hanging lights.
Tel: 800 944 2233
www.dwr.com

IKEA
Affordable lighting, including track and spotlights
Tel: 516 681 4532
www.ikea-usa.com

LIGHTING STORE USA
All kinds of lighting fixtures and contemporary lamps. Available online only.
www.lightingstoreusa.com

RUTH'S LAMPS AND SHADES, INC.
Custom made lampshades in a variety of styles and fabrics.
Tel: 215 836 1101
www.ruthslampsandshades.com

SHADES OF LIGHT
Table and floor lamps, ceiling fixtures, sconces, chandeliers, and more.
Tel: 800 262 6612
www.shades-of-light.com

VINTAGE LIGHTING
Rewired and restored fixtures of electric, converted gas and combination lighting.
Tel: 705 742 8078
www.vintagelighting.com

BERCELI
Wide range of products for the kitchen, including cabinets and tempered glass sinks.
Tel: 877 9 berceli
www.berceli.com

**CANYON CREEK
CABINET COMPANY**
Cabinets and islands built just for you. Choice of woods and custom design.
Tel: 228 0801
www.canyoncreek.com

CROWN POINT
Several styles including Shaker, Arts and Crafts, Milk Paint, and Victorian.
Tel: 800 000 4994
www.crown-point.com

HAAS CABINET CO., INC.
Custom cabinets for the entire home built to your specifications in a choice of woods.
Tel: 800 457 6458
www.haascabinets.com

IKEA
Value-for-money fitted and modular units in modern styles.
Tel: 516 681 4532
www.ikea-usa.com

KENNEBEC COMPANY
Period and handcrafted wood cabinets.
Tel: 207 443 2131
www.kennebeccompany.com

KITCHENCRAFT CABINETS
Different woods and designer selections of cabinet doors and kitchens. In Canada.
Tel: 800 463 9707
www.kitchencraft.com

KRAFTMADE
Built-to-order cabinets for every room in your home.
Tel: 888 562 7744
www.kraftmade.com

LOWES
Has everything you could need for a kitchen makeover.
Tel: 800 44 LOWES
www.lowes.com

MILLS PRIDE
Allows you to design your kitchen online.
Tel: 800 441 0337
www.millspride.com

STUDIO BECKER
Wood cabinets for your entire home.
Tel: 510 865 1616
www.studiobecker.com

STORAGE AND ACCESSORIES

BANANA REPUBLIC
The popular clothier brings its elegance and style to the bath.
Tel: 888 277 8953
www.bananarepublic.com

BED BATH AND BEYOND
Towels, bathmats and toothbrush holders. All your bathroom needs in popular styles and colors.
Tel: 800 GO BEYOND
www.bedbathandbeyond.com

BLOOMINGDALES
Towels, bathrobes and bedroom slippers.
Tel: 800 472 0788
www.bloomingdales.com

CONCINNITY
Towel racks, glass and metal storage shelves and mirrors.
Tel: 800 356 9993
www.concinnity-usa.com

CRATE AND BARREL
Towel racks, toothbrush holders, storage and more.
Tel: 800 967 6696
www.crateandbarrel.com

FRONT GATE
Bath towels in many hues, toothbrush holders, towel racks and other bathroom accessories.
Tel: 800 626 6488
www.frontgate.com

HAMMACHER SCHLEMMER
Anti-microbial shower curtains, standing and hanging towel racks and other bathroom needs.
Tel: 800 321 1484
www.hammacher.com

IKEA
Freestanding storage units and wall-mounted fittings in a range of finishes, from country pine to modern metal and glass.
Tel: 516 681 4532
www.ikea-usa.com

JC PENNEY
Towels, shower curtains, shower caddies, shelves and more.
Tel: 800 222 6161
www.jcpenney.com

LINENS'N THINGS
Affordable brand name towels and other bath products.
Tel: 866 568 7378
www.lnt.com

MACYS
Bathrobes and bath towels
as well as slippers and
toothbrush holders.
Tel: 800 BUY MACY
www.macys.com

THE NATURAL
A collection of brass and iron
towel racks and other bathroom fixtures.
Tel: 888 253 6466
www.widerview.com

PLOW AND HEARTH
Country-style accents for
the bathroom.
Tel: 800 494 7544
www.plowhearth.com

RESTORATION HARDWARE
Towel racks, toilet paper
holders and other bathroom
supplies.
Tel: 800 762 1005
www.restorationhardware.com

SILVO HOME
Medicine cabinets, shower
caddies, towel racks and more.
Tel: 800 331 1261
www.silvo.com

SMEDBO
Metal and wall mounted towel
and bathrobe racks.
Tel: 847 615 0000
www.smedco.se/us

SPIEGEL
Bathware, towels and
bathrobes all in one
convenient place.
Tel: 800 527 1577
www.spiegel.com

STACKS AND STACKS
Bath pillows, bathmats, shower
caddies, storage and more.
Tel: 800 761 5222
www.stacksandstacks.com

STROUDS
Towels, bathmats, toothbrush-
holders and other bathroom
conveniences.
Tel: 800 STROUDS
www.strouds.com

TARGET
Inexpensive source for fun,
colorful bath towels, bathrobes
and other bathroom products,
even a toothbrush.
Tel: 800 800 8800
www.target.com

STORAGE AND ACCESSORIES

ADVICE

ACE HARDWARE
Helpful advice for painting, installations, working with tools, lighting and electrical equipment.
Tel: 630 990 6600
www.acehardware.com

BENJAMIN MOORE
Helpful tips for painting and getting the decorative effects you want.
Tel: 800 344 0400
www.benjaminmoore.com

BETTER HOMES AND GARDENS
Advice on decorating and arranging all the rooms in the house from the magazine experts.
www.bhg.com

CONSUMER REPORTS
Reports on all major appliances and nearly all brand name products, including mattresses.
www.consumerreports.org

HOME DEPOT
Helpful tips for paintings, putting in bathroom fixtures and lighting and more.
Tel: 800 430 3376
www.homedepot.com

HOME FURNISH.COM
Advice on picking out bedroom furniture and mattresses, as well as finding the right sized mattress for your room.
www.homefurnish.com

STENCIL ARTISANS LEAGUE, INC.
Helpful stencil tips, where to find the best designs and more.
Tel: 505 865 9119
www.sali.com